Choosing Virtue in a Changing World

A New Look at the Seven Deadly Sins

Daniel L. Lowery, C.SS.R.

LIGUORI
PUBLICATIONS

One Liguori Drive
Liguori, Missouri 63057-9999
(314) 464-2500

Imprimi Potest:
James Shea, C.SS.R.
Provincial, St. Louis Province
The Redemptorists

Imprimatur:
Most Rev. Edward J. O'Donnell, D.D., V.G.
Auxiliary Bishop
Archdiocese of St. Louis

ISBN 0-89243-324-8
Library of Congress Catalog Card Number: 90-60737

Scripture selections are taken from the NEW AMERICAN BIBLE WITH REVISED NEW TESTAMENT, copyright © 1986, by the Confraternity of Christian Doctrine, Washington, DC 20017, and are used by permission of copyright owner. All rights reserved.

Excerpts from *Economic Justice for All,* copyright © 1986, United States Catholic Conference (USCC), Washington, DC, are used with permission. All rights reserved.

Excerpts reprinted with permission from *U.S. Catholic,* published by Claretian Publications, 205 West Monroe, Chicago, IL 60606.

Excerpts from *Deadly Sins and Saving Virtues* by Donald Capps, copyright © 1987, Fortress Press, 426 S. Fifth Street, Minneapolis, MN 55440, are reprinted with permission.

Excerpts from *Whatever Became of Sin?* by Karl Menninger, copyright © 1973, E.P. Dutton Publishers, 375 Hudson Street, Third Floor, New York, NY 10014, are used with permission.

Excerpts from *The Seven Deadly Sins Today* by Henry Fairlie, copyright © 1979, by the University of Notre Dame Press, are reprinted with permission.

Contents

Foreword

While I was working on this booklet, a young couple stopped by my office to say hello. My word processor was "hot," and my notes were scattered across my desk. They asked me what I was working on, and I told them I was preparing a booklet on the seven deadly sins and the seven life-giving virtues. I could tell from their reaction that they didn't have the slightest idea of what I was talking about!

This did not really surprise me. I'm sure that many other people of their age group, and even older, would have the same reaction. Yet it was not too long ago (thirty...forty years?) that most Catholics learned about the seven deadly sins, or capital sins, from preachers and teachers. Many people even memorized them. They were considered a handy tool for moral instruction and examination of conscience.

Then, for a variety of reasons, there was a period of time when this approach to Christian morality fell into disfavor and not much was heard of it. The young couple mentioned above certainly had good religious training, but that training did not include a formal treatment of the seven deadly sins.

In recent times, however, there has been a resurgence of interest in these sins and in the virtues that stand in opposition to them. Many religious educators and spiritual directors believe that an understanding of the seven deadly sins and the seven life-giving virtues can be as helpful to modern Christians as they were to our ancestors in the faith. In the past ten or so years a number of books and articles have emerged to update this dimension of Christian morality. This booklet takes its place among them.

Realizing that many people today are not familiar with this subject matter, I offer in chapter one of this booklet a brief history of these deadly, or capital, sins; why they are considered important; and how the corresponding virtues can aid us in our imitation of Christ.

After that a chapter is devoted to each of the deadly sins and their corresponding life-giving virtues in this order: Pride/Humility, Envy/Love, Anger/Meekness, Sloth/Joy, Avarice/Poverty, Gluttony/Temperance, Lust/Chastity.

The title of this booklet is *Choosing Virtue in a Changing World*. Change has certainly become a normal part of almost every area of our lives, including the area of morality. In time of change, especially in morality, we need strong convictions and principles about right and wrong. I believe that a serious reflection on the deadly sins and life-giving virtues can provide such a foundation for us as we try to remain faithful to Christian values.

To assist those who use this booklet, I have supplied some reflection/discussion questions at the end of each chapter. I hope that these might make the material more practical for individuals or groups. In addition I have included a selected bibliography at the end of this booklet.

I wish to thank my friend and colleague, David Polek, C.SS.R., and his staff at Liguori Publications for encouraging me to undertake this work and for their kind assistance in many different ways.

I hope that those who read this booklet will come to a better knowledge and a deeper love of Christian values in a changing world.

Daniel L. Lowery, C.SS.R.

CHAPTER ONE

Deadly Sins

"Sin is lawlessness."

(1 JOHN 3:4)

Life-giving Virtues

"Put on the new self."

(EPHESIANS 4:24)

In 1974 I was returning from Rome to New York on a widebodied plane. We boarded the plane at nine o'clock in the morning. I had a window seat. The man who sat next to me looked to be about thirty years old.

Experienced travelers, I have noticed, often play it cool at the start of a long trip. As soon as they get settled and attach their seat belt, they immediately begin working on reports or reading a book. They bury their head in what they are doing, reluctant to strike up a conversation. They seem to fear that they might get caught in an endless conversation about things they aren't interested in.

On this particular day I immediately began reviewing some notes from the meeting I had attended in Rome. My seatmate immediately began reading a hardcover book he had taken from his briefcase. I noticed the title of the book; I had never heard of it but was intrigued by it: *The First Deadly Sin* by Lawrence Sanders.

Several hours later, when lunch was being served, my seatmate and I struck up a conversation. His name was Tom; he was from Detroit; he had been in Rome for a week-long business meeting. When he discovered I was a Catholic priest, he told me that he too was a Catholic and had attended Catholic grade school and high school.

Apparently he was as intrigued by the title of his book as I was. He said, "I always enjoyed religion classes in school, and I took them seriously. I've always prided myself on being pretty well informed about religious matters. But I never remember hearing anything about 'deadly sins.' I wonder if I missed something — or is this expression not common among Catholics?" I told Tom that I might be able to jog his memory. "Did you ever hear of the 'seven capital sins'?" I asked him. Sure enough, that phrase meant something to him. "Yes," he said, "and I think I know what they are." He told me that when he was a senior in high school, his class went to a Jesuit retreat house for a special midweek retreat. The preacher of the retreat told the group that the theme of his talks could be remembered by a mnemonic: PALE GAS. As it turned out, the retreat was about the seven capital sins: Pride, Anger, Lust, Envy, Gluttony, Avarice and Sloth.

I explained to Tom that these were indeed the sins or vices that were traditionally called the "capital sins." More recently, however, these same sins or vices were commonly referred to as the "deadly sins." Most people today, and especially publishers, seem to think that "deadly" is a word more likely to capture the attention of the public than the word *capital*. Tom and I agreed that this was probably true.

This conversation took place, mind you, before Lawrence Sanders published novels not only about the first deadly sin but about several others as well. It may be that this widely read novelist has done more to make "deadly sins" a part of our common vocabulary than any other person!

DEADLY SINS

It is not entirely clear how the term "deadly sins" developed. In this context "deadly" is not just another word for "mortal," because these sins are not necessarily mortal sins, at least as that term is understood in Catholic theology. It may be that they were considered deadly because many of the actions flowing from them were destructive; in a spiritual sense these sins bring forth death rather than life.

The term "capital sins," on the other hand, has a long history. While these particular sins are not neatly categorized in the Bible, all of them are mentioned there in various ways, as will be seen. In the Christian tradition the capital sins were first cataloged by the Fathers of the desert. Writing toward the end of the second century, John Cassian spoke of the capital sins in his conferences to the monks. More than any other single person, however, Saint Gregory the Great (540 to 604) was the author who in his *Book of Morals* really popularized the idea of the capital sins, offering a list of them that was slightly different from the way they are often listed today.

Saint Thomas Aquinas (1225-1274), with his usual thoroughness, treated the capital sins in his masterful work known as the *Summa Theologica*. (Saint Thomas will be quoted frequently in this book.) What is especially noteworthy about his treatment is that he also treats the "capital virtues." In other words he not only tells us what is wrong but also how it can be made right.

It is clear that in the winding course of Christian spirituality

11

the specific number of capital sins has varied. Theologian Bernard Häring suggests that in the first letter of John only three are mentioned: "For all that is in the world, sensual lust, enticement for the eyes, and a pretentious life, is not from the Father but is from the world" (1 John 2:16). During the monastic period, eight sins were often listed, but eventually theologians settled on seven. There were various reasons for this, but one that is especially intriguing is described by Donald Capps.

He points out that "the seven-day week may have had something to do with it. A list of seven sins would lend itself to daily prayer, with each day's prayer focusing on the sin assigned to it."[1] He goes on to say that Sunday is the day we combat pride by proclaiming God, not ourselves, as the center of creation. Envy is Monday's sin and anger is Tuesday's sin; both of these involve a struggle against our wounded "self" and require a continuation of Sunday's struggle against pride. Sloth is Wednesday's sin: At midpoint between Sundays we are most susceptible to spiritual indifference. Greed and gluttony, Thursday's and Friday's sins, are the sins of self-indulgence that follow from the previous day's loss of spiritual fortitude. These two sins culminate in lust, Saturday's sin, which is at its deadliest on the last day of the week when the spiritual effects of Sunday are at their lowest ebb.

During the Middle Ages, many Christian authors and preachers often turned their attention to a treatment of the seven deadly sins. They were a standard part of religious education and often used as sermon topics. (Unfortunately, the sins often received more attention than the virtues to which they were opposed.) They even made their way into religious art and literature. For instance, Dante Alighieri (1265-1321) used them in his depiction of purgatory. Geoffrey Chaucer (1340-1400), who is best known for *The Canter-*

bury Tales, featured a story called "The Parson's Tale" in which he wrote: "At the root then of these seven sins is Pride, the general root of all evils; for from this root spring certain branches, as Envy, Wrath [Anger], Sloth, Avarice [Covetousness], Gluttony, and Lechery [Lust]."

Cold Sins, Hot Sins

It is worth noticing the order in which these deadly sins are listed. The one given by Chaucer is favored by Saint Gregory and by most of the great theologians of the Middle Ages. In more recent times, because of various reasons (for example, the mnemonic mentioned above!), the order is often changed around. Obviously, this arrangement is not a divine revelation written on stone tablets, but the traditional one focuses our attention on an important point.

Henry Fairlie makes this point with great clarity when he says that "all the Seven Deadly Sins are demonstrations of love that has gone wrong....Pride and Envy and Anger are sins of *perverted* love. The love is directed to a worthy object — in each case, to oneself — but it is directed in a false manner. The fault in this is that one imagines that one may gain some good for oneself by causing harm to others." Passing over sloth for the moment, he discusses the last three sins in the lineup: "Avarice and Gluttony and Lust are sins of *excessive* love. The love may again be directed to what in themselves are deserving objects, but it is so excessive that it interrupts, and must in the end destroy, one's capacity to love other objects that are also and perhaps even more deserving."[2]

Another point worth noticing is the distinction often made in moral theology between "sins of malice" and "sins of weakness." The sins of malice are the "cold" sins: that is, those in which self-centeredness is so paramount and so perverse that it strikes out at others in a cool and calculating manner. The sins of weakness, on the other hand, are the "hot" sins: that is, those which stem from passions and feelings that are out of control. The cold sins are marked by hardness of heart; the warm sins indicate self-gratification. This is not to imply, of course, that hot sins are gentle and harmless. They can be as destructive of self and others as the cold sins. What is helpful about this distinction is that it helps to trace the deep roots of sinful acts and gives clues on how to dig up these roots.

Sins or PALS?

In the course of time, the theme of the capital sins lost some of its attractiveness for preachers and writers. One reason for this was that this approach seemed too negative for many people. The tendency was to place great emphasis on the sins or vices and very little on the positive virtues or values. Recently, however, as mentioned in the Foreword, the pendulum seems to have swung back, and once again there are a number of books and articles being written about the seven deadly sins.

This renewed interest may stem from the concern of many people that our society is losing its moral bearings, dismissing both virtue and vice as irrelevant. In his popular book, *Whatever Became of Sin?* the highly respected psychiatrist Karl Menninger challenged Americans to recover the language of sin and guilt. In one of the chapters of his book entitled "The Old Seven Deadly Sins (And Some New Ones)," Menninger insists that the real problem is not simply the individual, external acts of sin but rather the deep attitudes that give rise to the sinful acts. The external acts "are samples of the behavior dictated by a wrong attitude, a hard heart, a cold heart, an evil heart."[3]

Another reason for renewed interest in the deadly sins is

awareness of the modern tendency to hide moral evil behind a barrage of newly coined words ("I misspoke" instead of "I lied") or to dismiss sin in a cloud of verbal puffery. In an imaginative article, Mary Ellen Ashcroft tells how she "took a tour of the advertising agency for marketing the seven deadly sins today." The CEO of the agency asked her: "Do you know what we do here?" She replied: "I understand you do the marketing for the Seven Deadly Sins." The CEO took offense at that. "Deadly is rather extreme, don't you think? Nuclear war is deadly. Cancer can become deadly. The habits that we promote are pleasant, fun, even healthy! We like to call them the Seven Pleasurable Alternative Life Styles — PALS for short."[4]

Deadly Fountainheads

Whether they are called deadly sins or capital sins, the titles themselves do not reveal much about these realities. Further study is needed on this subject.

First, as mentioned above, the word *sin* here is used not so much in the sense of a specific thought, word, or deed against the law of God but rather in the sense of an habitual pattern of evil which in its turn gives rise to specific acts. For example, the capital sin of anger may be the source or the root from which spring many particular acts of impatience, detraction, rash judgment, and the like.

Second, the word *capital* comes from the Latin word *caput*, meaning "head." The capital sins are like fountainheads from which many small streams flow. Or, to use the image of Saint Gregory, they are like leaders of armies with many individual soldiers trailing after them. Similarly, Chaucer calls them "captains" inasmuch as "they are...the sources of all other sins." Thus, Saint Thomas points out: "In this sense a capital sin or vice is one from which other vices arise." For example,

15

sloth is a kind of spiritual laziness or boredom in regard to the things of God. From this fountainhead may flow the neglect of prayer and worship, disregard for the works of mercy or the spirit of sacrifice, an exaggerated seeking of personal ease and comfort.

It seems clear, therefore, that the tradition of the capital sins provides us with a helpful tool to trace patterns of sinfulness in our lives. This tradition, as Urban Voll indicates, can help "to make a diagnosis of apparently unrelated symptoms under which lies the core of spiritual disease."[5] We may begin to see, for example, not only individual acts of envy but rather the roots of envy in our lives. That can be very helpful in developing our spiritual life.

LIFE-GIVING VIRTUES

It would certainly be a big mistake to concentrate only on the seven capital sins while disregarding the virtues which are their opposites. A constant reflection on the roots of sin in us can be very discouraging unless it is accompanied by insights into how we can become better Christians. That is why Saint Thomas' treatment of the capital sins is accompanied by a treatment of the "capital virtues." And that is the approach we want to take in this booklet. We will first examine what the capital sin means to us and how it may affect our lives; and then we will turn to the corresponding virtue which will help us to overcome the capital sin.

Before looking at the various facets of the deadly sins and their corresponding virtues, however, we might take a longer look at the overall importance of virtues in our Christian lives. As Christians, we are called to imitate the life and spirit of Jesus Christ, to "put on the new self, created in God's way in righteousness and holiness of truth" (Ephesians 4:24). According to the Catholic tradition, the three theological (God-given and God-directed) virtues of faith, hope, and charity are pure gifts of grace: gifts of God given to us with sanctifying grace so that we can live and act on the supernatural level. At the same time, the moral virtues, many and varied as they are, are gifts that enable us to shape our conscious behavior according to the law of God as revealed by Jesus.

The imitation of Christ, to which we are called by grace, should happen not merely in theory, in our minds, but also in our lives, in our ways of acting and reacting. "By their fruits you will know them" (Matthew 7:16). In the gospels Jesus speaks often about basic values: compassion, forgiveness, mutual charity, justice, self-sacrifice. A Christian virtue may be described as an habitual way of acting in accord with these values. A vice is an habitual way of acting in opposition to these values. Our growth in the Christian life, in our imitation of Christ, will in part come about by our practice of the Christian virtues and our triumph over the opposite vices.

Morality of the Heart

Yet we also want to avoid the mistake of thinking that our imitation of Christ consists merely in external acts of virtue. In his many clashes with the Pharisees, Jesus rejected their morality "of the law" and insisted on a "morality of the heart." Jesus accused the Pharisees of putting their man-made traditions and practices above the law of God (see Matthew 15:1-10). He faulted them for placing heavy burdens on the shoulders of ordinary people while not lifting a finger to help lighten their burdens (see Matthew 23:4). He warned them about doing good deeds simply to attract the attention of others (see Matthew 6:1-6).

In contrast to this Pharisaic morality, Jesus underlined the interior dispositions of mind and heart and will. To Jesus the internal motive from which an action springs is more significant than the external act itself. Jesus spells out this theme in clear and down-to-earth language when, for example, he says to the people:

"Hear and understand. It is not what enters one's mouth that defiles that person; but what comes out of the mouth is what defiles one."…"Do you not realize that everything that enters the mouth passes into the stomach and is expelled…? But the things that come out of the mouth come from the heart, and they defile. For from the heart come evil thoughts, murder, adultery, unchastity, theft, false witness, blasphemy. These are what defile a person, but to eat with unwashed hands does not defile."

(Matthew 15:10-11, 17-20)

This teaching of Jesus challenges all of us to practice virtues and avoid vices not merely in an external, face-saving way, but more fully in a genuine desire to imitate Christ and live by his gospel. We must not forget that vices occur first in our hearts, secondly in our actions. Anger, for example, is often expressed in external actions, but it begins in the profound depths of our hearts where hatred or disrespect or resentment grow unchecked. Lust, as experience testifies, may be expressed in many ways, but it is embraced spiritually, in the heart, before it is manifested physically in our behavior.

In this booklet we want courageously to look at the roots of evil — the deadly or capital sins — as we experience them in our hearts and in our lives. We want to root them out by enshrining in our hearts and in our lives the life-giving and growth-producing virtues that Jesus manifested to us in his teaching and, even more powerfully, in his example.

Reflection/Discussion Questions

1. After reading this chapter, which of the images used by theologians is most helpful to you in understanding a deadly, or capital, sin? Do you have any fresh image that might be helpful?
2. Is the distinction between "cold sins" and "hot sins" meaningful to you? If so, can you think of concrete examples of each?
3. How do you feel about the statement "that our society is losing its moral bearings, dismissing both virtue and vice as irrelevant"? Why do you agree or disagree?
4. Write out or explain orally your understanding of Jesus' teaching on "the morality of the heart" as opposed to "the morality of the law." Does this teaching affect your life in any concrete way?

NOTES

[1]Donald Capps, *Deadly Sins and Saving Virtues,* (Philadelphia: Fortress, 1987), p. 12.

[2]Henry Fairlie, *The Seven Deadly Sins Today,* (Notre Dame: University of Notre Dame Press, 1979), p. 35-36.

[3]Karl Menninger, *Whatever Became of Sin?* (New York: E.P. Dutton Publishers), hardcover, p. 172.

[4]Mary Ellen Ashcroft, "Are the Seven Deadly Sins Still Deadly?" *New Covenant*, September 1989, p. 9.

[5]Urban Voll, "Capital Sins," *New Catholic Encyclopedia*.

CHAPTER TWO

Pride

"You will be like gods."

(GENESIS 3:5)

Humility

"Humble yourselves before the Lord."

(JAMES 4:10)

T he group was having a discussion at Holy Spirit Retreat Center. Father Michael had given a presentation on self-love and self-esteem.

Lorne was the first to speak: "I have good reasons for self-esteem. I've worked hard and pushed myself. I have been very successful. And I have a lot of good things to show for it."

Eugene said: "I really feel good about myself these days. I have become aware of my gifts and talents. I have a much better self-image. It wasn't always like this. For years I suffered from low self-esteem. I really didn't love myself. But now I do."

After a pause Kathy spoke: "I am really happy about my ability to sing. It used to be that I couldn't accept a compliment; I felt that people were complimenting me just to make me feel good. But now I accept their praise graciously because I know I sing well, and I am happy about it."

Are Lorne and Eugene and Kathy guilty of the sin of pride? Or are they showing forth the virtue of humility? Is pride always sinful? Is pride never sinful? What do we mean by pride anyway? The Christian tradition, properly understood, offers answers to these questions. Here is a look at some of the answers.

PRIDE

The sin of pride can be understood in two ways. In one sense it is not a particular sin but rather the root of all sin and the strongest influence propelling us to sin. In another sense it is a particular sin, one of the capital, or deadly, sins.

Saint Gregory did not include pride among the seven deadly sins. Rather, he characterized it as the sovereign of all sins: "Pride, the sovereign of vices, when it has captured and vanquished the heart, forthwith delivers it into the hands of its lieutenants, the seven capital vices, that they may despoil it and produce vices of all kinds."

Back to the Garden

Pride as the root of all sin goes back to the Garden of Eden. In the story of humankind's fall from grace, the true face of pride is shown. "It is evident," says Saint Thomas, "that our first sin was pride."

In Genesis we read:

The serpent asked the woman, "Did God really tell you not to eat from any of the trees in the garden?" The woman answered the serpent: "We may eat of the fruit of the trees in the garden; it is only about the fruit of the tree in the middle of the garden that God said, 'You shall not eat it or even touch it, lest you die.' " But the serpent said to the woman: "You certainly will not die! No, God knows well that the moment you eat of it your eyes will be opened and you will be like gods who know what is good and what is bad."

(Genesis 3:1-5)

Commenting on this text, the Jerusalem Bible lucidly explains that the knowledge Adam sought here "is the power of deciding for himself what is good and what is evil and of acting accordingly, a claim to complete moral independence by which man refuses to recognize his status as a created being. The first sin was an attack on God's sovereignty, a sin of pride. The rebellion is described in concrete terms as the transgression of an express command of God for which the text uses the image of a forbidden fruit."

In its own way, every real sin is likewise an attack against God's sovereignty, a rebellion of the creature against the Creator, a transgression of God's law and God's will.

> The beginning of pride is man's stubbornness
>   in withdrawing his heart from his Maker.

(Sirach 10:12)

As Ralph Martin has pointed out, "The core perversion that afflicts the human race is not sex or money or power. It is rebellion — rejection of God's authority and plan, the refusal to submit to God and accept his truth."[1] It is in that sense that pride is the root of all sin and the strongest influence propelling men and women to sin.

Self-centeredness

As a particular sin, pride may be described as a disordered love of self by which a person takes individual credit for what are actually gifts of God and by which a person seeks unreasonable acclaim for personal accomplishments. Pride springs from an exaggerated egocentrism or self-centeredness. Of course, there is a self-love that is good and virtuous. But in pride a person makes "self" absolute and central, isolating self from God and others, or using others for the achievement of selfish purposes.

An almost infallible sign of pride is isolationism. Exaggerated self-centeredness dismisses the need for community with others. The proud person is apt to be aloof and distant from others, arrogant and condescending, except of course when a false show of cooperation is in his or her best interest. The proud person is rarely concerned about "we," but always about "me, myself, and I." The proud person lives by a code of self-sufficiency and uses others to blow up the hot-air balloon of self.

Lorne, who spoke at the beginning of this chapter, is a good example of this self-centeredness. Every one of his sentences begins with "I." There is no "we" to be found. It is almost certain that Lorne arrived at his present level of success with the help of others: parents, spouse, teachers, partners. But Lorne has managed to disregard the assistance of others in his overwhelming need to take all the credit for his isolated self.

Many sins — such as boasting, arrogance, vanity, hard-heartedness — flow from the deadly sin of pride.

For pride is the reservoir of sin,
    a source which runs over with vice.

(Sirach 10:13)

Pride manifests itself in many sinful ways. In an informal discussion of pride, a group of men and women discussed the following camouflages that pride uses.

- **The lord of the manor:** This describes the kind of people who have never learned how to exercise authority. Whether in the home, the workplace, the church, such men or women will, in the words of Jesus, "lord it over others, making their importance felt." Far from caring about the welfare of those subject to them, these "authority figures" dismiss the good of others as they relentlessly seek their own.
- **The show-off:** This describes the kind of adults who, like spoiled children, indulge in vanity and seek self-importance in externals such as clothes, furniture, cars. In their own inflated opinion, whatever they own or use must be better (and seen to be better) than what someone else has. Such people, as ridiculous as it often seems, strut around as if they were God's gift to creation.
- **The put-down artist:** This describes those arrogant persons who seek to be "higher" by making other people "lower"; who seek to be "number one" by making sure that others are at least "number two." "Pride must be competitive, since it cannot bear to concede first place to anyone else, even when its real needs are satisfied."[2] Such persons are incapable of appreciating the gifts of others because they are always seen as a diminishment of their own gifts.
- **The know-it-all:** These persons are "wise in their own conceits." They consider their opinions, once formed, absolutely unchangeable and superior to everyone else's. Such people are typically full of prejudice against other races, creeds, and groups. They are usually close-minded and judgmental. In addition they are, as a rule, gigantic bores.
- **The supersensitive soul:** These people hide their pride behind the mask of "hurt feelings." Those who live or work with such people must "walk on eggs," lest their feelings

be bruised. The supersensitive are constantly seeking apologies from those who have "offended" them. In reality this is another way of attracting attention to themselves and getting their own way.

Pride is a pervasive sin and a persistent one. Like a roaring lion, it goes about seeking whom it may devour. Christians who want to tame this beast will have to stand on guard and use all the tools at their disposal. One very important tool is the virtue of humility.

HUMILITY

Humility is not one of the all-time favorite virtues of modern Christians; many of them would be embarrassed to mention it. It's usually considered a negative virtue rather than a positive one, repressive rather than liberating. This may be partly because the virtue of humility is widely misunderstood. Modern references to humility are almost always associated with "wimps" or "milksops."

Whatever be the case, there is no doubt that the early Christian community, just as it saw pride as the root of all evil, so saw humility as the foundation of the whole edifice of Christian virtue. Theologian Bernard Häring does not hesitate to say: "Christian thought and practice has always looked upon it [humility] as a fundamental virtue serving as the foundation of the whole edifice of Christian virtue."[3]

Thomas Merton, the Trappist monk whose spiritual vision was so startlingly clear, goes a step further: "It is almost impossible to overestimate the value of true humility and its power in the spiritual life....Humility contains in itself the answer to all the great problems of the life of the soul."[4]

Humility Is Truth

What is humility? One of the best-known answers to that question is the answer of Saint Theresa of Avila: "Humility is truth." That is, to be sure, an excellent definition, provided we understand it. But to do that, we have to break it into two parts. Humility is truth in self-understanding and truth in action.

Humility is truth in self-understanding. This is the heart of the matter. This is where humility is shown as the direct opposite of pride. It means that we have a genuine awareness of our human condition as creatures of God. It means that we make no pretense to be "like gods." It means that we are happily convinced of this most basic truth about ourselves: that God is the Creator and the Source of our life and our gifts.

> "The God who made the world and all that is in it, the Lord of heaven and earth, does not dwell in sanctuaries made by human hands, nor is he served by human hands because he needs anything. Rather it is he who gives to everyone life and breath and everything.... 'In him we live and move and have our being....' "
>
> (Acts 17:24-25, 28)

In the confrontations between Jesus and the Pharisees, we see how the Pharisees had come to believe that they were somehow the creators of their own virtue and grace and justification before God. Jesus challenged this.

He then spoke this parable addressed to those who believed in their own self-righteousness while holding everyone else in contempt:

26

"Two people went up to the temple area to pray; one was a Pharisee and the other was a tax collector. The Pharisee took up his position and spoke this prayer to himself, 'O God, I thank you that I am not like the rest of humanity — greedy, dishonest, adulterous — or even like this tax collector. I fast twice a week, and I pay tithes on my whole income.' But the tax collector stood off at a distance and would not even raise his eyes to heaven but beat his breast and prayed, 'O God, be merciful to me a sinner.' I tell you, the latter went home justified, not the former; for everyone who exalts himself will be humbled, and the one who humbles himself will be exalted."

(Luke 18:10-14)

In this classic parable — a short story with a punch line — we see how often the Pharisee uses "I." He did not so much offer a prayer as recite a list of reasons why he was better than everyone else. The Pharisee was "self-righteous" and believed that his good works justified him in the sight of God. The tax collector, aware of his sinfulness, realized that he had no reason for self-justification and had no choice but to depend upon the gracious mercy of God. From this simple parable Jesus draws an all-embracing conclusion: "For everyone who exalts himself will be humbled, and the one who humbles himself will be exalted." The most basic truth about ourselves is that every gift and talent we have comes to us from the creative hand of God. Truth in self-knowledge asks only that we remember this. Humility does not demand that we deny our goodness, our gifts, our talents. It demands only that we acknowledge where they came from. The theme song of the humble person could well be: "Who confers distinction upon you? What do you possess that you have not received? But if you have received it, why are you boasting as if you did not receive it?" (1 Corinthians 4:7).

Returning to the discussion at the Holy Spirit Retreat Center mentioned at the beginning of this chapter, were Eugene and Kathy guilty of pride? Or were they showing forth the virtue of humility?

Unfortunately, the word *pride* is often used to describe persons who have a positive sense of their dignity and worth or a pleased satisfaction in their gifts and achievements. Used in this sense, pride is certainly not sinful. It is a kind of heresy to think that true self-love is necessarily motivated by pride.

We must make a sharp distinction between true self-love on the one hand and exaggerated self-centeredness on the other. True self-love means that we believe and accept a profound truth about ourselves: namely, that we are made in the image and likeness of God, are profoundly loved by God, and lavishly gifted by God. We can love ourselves not for false reasons but for the best of all reasons. Provided we recognize that our goodness comes from God, we are practicing humility in acknowledging it.

Humility is also truth in action. This implies that our basic convictions about ourselves and our abilities and talents affect our manner, our speech, our association with others. Our entire manner will indicate that whatever talents we have are gifts of God. That is the truth and we are happy to live in accord with it. We do not, therefore, put on airs or belittle others or put them down. We don't have to. We know the truth and the truth sets us free!

Freedom is indeed one of the fruits of humility: freedom from the tyranny of false images, from the petty conflicts of envy and jealousy, from the vain struggle to be what we are not. Dom Hubert Van Zeller reminds us that the humble can afford to be supremely unconcerned about many of the things that upset the proud. They do not waste time in trying to create an impression or in worrying when they cannot get what they want.

Peace, too, is a fruit of humility. Inner peace comes when fear is overcome. Humility teaches us that we have nothing to fear, that God loves us and cares about us and has gifted us. Humility teaches us that we are not isolated individuals, having always to fend off hostile others, but rather are part of a community where people can accept one another as they are and support one another in their various gifts. Thomas Merton remarks that "a humble man is not afraid of failure. In fact, he is not afraid of anything, even of himself, since perfect humility implies confidence in the power of God, before whom no other power has any meaning and from whom there is no such thing as an obstacle."[5]

Yet, even though proud people are not widely loved, and even though humility holds out to us the blessed promises of freedom and peace, it is hard to commit ourselves to it. There is always the fear lurking in the back of our minds that others may take advantage of us or walk all over us. There is always the nagging doubt that we may be forgotten, passed over, unrecognized. What we forget, of course, is that humility gives us a whole new perspective on life. It takes the sting out of many things that used to hurt us. It brings a contentment, a simple joy, a way of using our gifts and accepting the gifts of others in a way that makes life happier than we thought it could be.

Reflection/Discussion Questions

1. What is your understanding of "original sin" as taught by the Church? How does it relate to pride?

2. How do you react to the five camouflages of pride as described in the text? Do you agree with them, disagree? Can you add any other examples from your experience?
3. In your own words, describe the virtue of humility. Do you think there is a difference between true humility and false humility? Explain.
4. Do you believe that humility leads to freedom and peace? If so, can you give any concrete examples from your own experience?

NOTES

[1]Ralph Martin, "Getting Free of Sexual Sin," *New Covenant*, April 1989, p. 14.

[2]Henry Fairlie, *The Seven Deadly Sins Today,* (Notre Dame: University of Notre Dame Press, 1979), p. 44.

[3]Bernard Häring, C.SS.R., *The Law of Christ,* (Westminster, Maryland: Newman Press, 1965) Volume 1, p. 547.

[4]Thomas Merton, *New Seeds of Contemplation,* (New York: New Direction Books, 1961), p. 181.

[5]Thomas Merton, the same, p. 190.

CHAPTER THREE

Envy

"Let us not be...envious of one another."

(GALATIANS 5:26)

Love

"Love...rejoices with the truth."

(1 CORINTHIANS 13:5-6)

It was fairly early on Monday morning. A young woman stood at the door of my office in the rectory. A boy of about four stood with her, holding her hand tightly. "Do you have a few minutes?" she asked. "Come in," I said.

Her name was Liz. She was thirty years old. She had two older children in addition to Michael, who was still holding on for dear life. Liz was an outgoing type of person, ready to say what was on her mind. "That sermon at Mass yesterday is still bugging me," she stated.

Our pastor had preached an insightful homily to our suburban community, challenging us to consider our values and priorities in the light of the gospel. Toward the end of the homily the pastor had posed several questions for us to consider: "What do you consider your predominant vice? Which sin has the tightest hold on you?"

"What really upsets me," said Liz, "is that my biggest fault is envy. Do you believe it? Here I am: I've got a loving husband with a good job, three healthy and happy kids, a nice house, a good car, all kinds of furniture, clothing, and food. You know, it's really hard for me to admit this, but sometimes when I take Michael for a walk through the neighborhood, I find myself full of envy for my neighbors…they all seem to have better houses, newer cars, smarter kids. I could kick myself."

Liz is certainly not alone. Dolores Curran, who writes with such clarity about Christian family life, asks the question: "Is envy still a deadly sin?" Her answer hits the nail on the head: "You bet. People envy families who get along with minimal friction. Adults envy other people's BMWs and VCRs. Teens covet Guess jeans and Reebok sneakers — to the point of making their peers envious and themselves miserable if they don't have the right labels hanging all over their bodies."[1]

It is a paradox that many people who live in the most affluent society on the face of the earth are nonetheless plagued by the deadly sin of envy. And, like Liz, many people find it hard to admit this. Envy seems so small-minded, so ugly, so shallow. "It has been said that envy is the one deadly sin to which no one readily confesses. It seems to be the nastiest, the most grim, the meanest. Sneering, sly, vicious, the face of envy is never lovely. It is never even faintly pleasant."[2] No wonder few people own up to it!

ENVY

While willing to admit that her biggest fault is envy, Liz did not seem particularly clear on just what constitutes envy. She could feel it but not define it. What is envy? Where does it come from?

The word *envy* seems to flow from two Latin words: *in* + *videre,* which might be translated as "to look askance at." *Webster's Seventh New Collegiate Dictionary* defines envy as "painful or resentful awareness of an advantage enjoyed by another joined with a desire to possess the same advantage." This definition reflects that of Chaucer, who describes envy as "sorrow at the prosperity of others and joy in their hurt."

Saint Thomas defines envy quite simply as "sorrow over another's good." Such a definition seems almost too simple to be helpful! But then Thomas adds a very important ingredient to our understanding of envy. He explains that the reason we grieve over another's good is that somehow we see that good as lessening our own value or excellence, somehow we see our neighbor's possessions as not only surpassing ours but also as taking away some of our prestige. For this reason, says Thomas, we are usually "envious of those goods about which people like to be honored or esteemed."

Several contemporary writers pick up on this important point made by Saint Thomas. Henry Fairlie, for example, describes envy in this way: "Envy is not merely a grieving on account of another's good...but a grieving because one regards that good as diminishing one's own and even as reflecting disgrace on oneself."[3] Donald Capps also points out that "envy forms when we believe that the other person's advantage or possession diminishes or brings disgrace on us. Once we believe that, we try to divest those we envy of their advantage, usually by trying to 'pull the other person down....' "[4]

Envy, as Dolores Curran pointed out, is often directed toward the material possessions of others. These are visible and tangible; they readily stir up the feelings of envy in us. But envy may also extend to resentment over spiritual gifts

33

and graces as well. There is an extreme form of spiritual envy whereby one person resents the very spiritual life of another. Theologians liken this to the sin against the Holy Spirit because it begrudges a brother or sister the very love and grace of God. More commonly perhaps, especially in close-knit parishes or prayer groups or religious communities, we find the kind of envy whereby some persons resent the special gifts or charisms of others, their reputation for being holy or close to God. As with envy of material possessions, so here too: The problem is not so much the gifts of other persons as it is the conviction that their spiritual richness somehow renders us spiritually poor.

Jealousy

In everyday situations we often use the words *envy* and *jealousy* interchangeably. We don't bother to make many distinctions about the strong feelings we experience. Envy and jealousy are certainly close relatives, but they are not identical. Envy is traditionally numbered among the deadly sins, as we have seen; if we were to add another sin to the list, it might well be jealousy.

Walter was a husky, good-looking young man, just ready to turn twenty. He was visibly upset as he talked to me. He told me that he had been going with a wonderful girl named Lori for about a year; he even hoped that someday they might get married. But Lori was quite upset with him. She said he was too jealous of her, and she didn't like it. Walter figured she was probably right but said he was totally confused about what jealousy was or where it came from or what to do about it.

Walter is certainly not alone. Like envy, jealousy is easy to feel but hard to define. Is there anyone, from the first-grader to the octogenarian, who has not felt the pangs of jealousy?

Some experts think that one way to get a handle on the meaning of jealousy is to compare it with envy. The comparison is not always neat and satisfying, but if we are content to paint with broad strokes, we can learn a lot from such a comparison.

What is jealousy? In general, jealousy has to do with persons. Envy is more concerned with things. Jealousy is a fear of losing another's exclusive or special love. Envy is sorrow over or a desire to possess what another has. Jealousy is resentment at being replaced by a rival. Envy is a kind of sadness over the good fortune of another because it somehow lessens our own stature. Understood in this way, Walter would be jealous of his girlfriend because he is afraid someone might steal her away from him. He would be envious of his neighbor's Cadillac or salary increase because his neighbor's possessions would seem to diminish Walter's worth.

The poet John Dryden once called jealousy "the jaundice of the soul." He was certainly right. Jealousy is a kind of spiritual sickness which easily turns trust to suspicion, love to hate, peace to fury. And it is a spreading sickness. It infects the jealous person, of course, but also the person who is the object of the jealousy. It may affect a good many other people as well.

Roots of Jealousy

Where does jealousy come from? It arises from fear and insecurity and immaturity. The jealous person is an immature person. Immaturity is marked by a preoccupation with self. Intense, unreasoning jealousy is a sure sign of immaturity. An old saying expresses it this way: "In jealousy there is more self-love than true love." Or, in the words of Saint Paul, "Love ...is not jealous" (1 Corinthians 13:4).

In the heady days of a young romance, a "little jealousy" is often considered cute. But the cuteness doesn't last, as any spouse or lover or friend who has been the object of jealousy readily knows. Jealousy is one of the most destructive of emotions. Sooner or later this green-eyed monster gobbles up all true love. Jealousy feeds on suspicion, erodes trust, arouses hostility. How many marriages and friendships have been broken on the shoals of jealousy? In the vivid image of Hubert Van Zeller, "jealousy finds a rosebush and leaves a stick."

Walter may be fortunate indeed that Lori has been so honest with him about the problem of jealousy. It may be that he can begin to learn how to control and channel his jealous feelings. Lori may be able to help by assuring him of her friendship and affection on one hand and reminding him of any undue possessiveness on the other. Together they may be able to keep the monster of jealousy at bay.

Cure for Jealousy

What can be done about jealousy? Unfortunately, there is no magic potion which will cure it. Jealous persons must begin by being ruthlessly honest with themselves. In addition, since there is a widespread impression that jealousy is an inborn trait about which individuals cannot do much, jealous persons must be firmly convinced that they can do something about it.

Jealousy must be seen for what it is: an unnecessary waste of something good, an unjustified spoiling of love and friendship. Jealous persons must drop the hundred-and-one excuses that "justify" their jealousy. The vice must be seen as a sickness. It needs surgery, not excuses.

Jealous persons must begin to deal with their immaturity. As persons and as Christians, they must choose in favor of growth by deciding to integrate Christian virtue into their real life. Jealous persons demand the center of the stage and the whole spotlight; each one must be at every moment "the one and only." Mature Christians, on the other hand, are humble, openhanded, and comfortable with allowing others their freedom, not graspingly possessive.

Jealous persons are forever suspicious, judgmental, intolerant. Mature Christians, on the other hand, try to be tolerant, trusting, peaceful. Jealous persons mistakenly think that they can demand affection or love. Mature Christians, on the other hand, know that love and affection are freely given gifts which should be received only with gratitude.

Jealous persons childishly think that they can push open the door of another's heart and demand entrance into another's life. Mature Christians know that love and friendship must be built slowly, trustingly, on a strong foundation; they recognize that in the house of love and friendship there will always be "sacred rooms" where even the friend and lover cannot go.

Envy (or jealousy, its close relative) is certainly a deadly sin. It has destroyed innumerable relationships. It is a spiritual sickness, not a cute ploy. Like all sins, it can of course be forgiven and healed — but only if the person recognizes the sickness in time and allows it to be touched by the healing grace of God.

LOVE

Obviously, envy (and jealousy, its counterpart) as described here, are sinful because they exhibit sorrow over what should make us rejoice — namely, our neighbor's good. Saint Thomas points out that "envy is contrary to love, whence the soul derives its spiritual life....Now both the object of love and the object of envy is the neighbor's good, but by contrary movements, since love rejoices in the neighbor's good, while envy grieves over it." To grieve over the good fortune and success of others is clearly a sin against Christian love. To take joy in the misfortune of others is perilously close to hatred.

Without doubt, envy is a violation of the great law of love which is the centerpiece of the teaching of Jesus. "This is my commandment: love one another as I love you....This I command you: love one another" (John 15:12, 17). Envy stands in stark contrast to the all-embracing love taught in Scripture: "See that no one returns evil for evil; rather, always seek what is good [both] for each other and for all" (1 Thessalonians 5:15). When envy edges toward real hatred — and perhaps it does more often than we realize — it falls under severe condemnation: "Everyone who hates his brother is a murderer, and you know that no murderer has eternal life remaining in him" (1 John 3:15).

The moral excellence of love in contrast to the malice of envy is also seen in envy's offspring. Saint Thomas says that envy gives birth to detraction and calumny (slander). Detraction means ruining another's reputation by making known, without a sufficiently serious reason, the hidden sins or failings of another. In detraction, what is said is true, but it is also secret and private. Calumny means the ruining of another's reputation by lies. It goes beyond detraction, of course, and is morally more offensive. In these ways envious persons strive to lower the reputation of another and so to raise their own. Envy will try anything to "pull the other person down."

Those who are trying to grow in the Christian life, therefore, must strive to overcome the deadly sin of envy by developing the life-giving virtue of love. In his famous "hymn to love," Saint Paul reminds us that true love does not seek its own interests...but rejoices in the truth (see 1 Corinthians

13:5-6). The truth is that our personal value and worth are conferred on us by a loving God; and purely material possessions, whether in our own hands or those of others, can neither substitute for that nor diminish it. Bernard Häring summarizes a lot of Christian wisdom when he advises: "The danger of the sin of envy is best met by meditation on the loving generosity of God toward all men and women...by childlike submission of self to the all-wise disposition of providence."[5] Saint Paul puts it even more simply: "If we live in the Spirit, let us also follow the Spirit. Let us not be...envious of one another" (Galatians 5:25-26).

True Self-love

Like all the deadly sins, envy has many layers. As we uncover one layer after the other, we begin to see that envy is not only opposed to love of neighbor, it is opposed to true self-love as well. To be sure, envy is often directed toward the material possessions of others, but its more basic concern may be our own self-worth and self-value. After all, if we draw our self-worth as persons from what we possess rather than from how we stand before God, we will naturally resent those who possess more than we because this fact in some way diminishes our dignity and value in our own eyes.

Perhaps envy is so common in our affluent society because many people do not really love themselves. "The envious man does not love himself, although he begins with self-love. He is not grateful for, or happy in, what he is or what he has. The sin is deadly, less because it destroys him than because it will not let him live. It will not let him live as himself, grateful for his qualities and talents, such as they are, and making the best and most rewarding use of them. His disparagement of others is a disparagement of himself; he regards himself with as much malice as he regards them."[6]

39

True self-love emerges when we believe and accept a profound truth about ourselves: namely, that we are made in the image and likeness of God, are profoundly loved by God and lavishly gifted by him. If such faith is the basis of our own self-love, envy of another's possessions will hardly be a problem. But if this foundation of true self-love is absent, then the demon of envy will see material possessions as conferring personal self-worth and will see the possessions of others as a threat to our own personhood. In that case it will be very difficult to practice the love of God above all and the love of our neighbor as ourselves.

Reflection/Discussion Questions

1. In your own words, how would you describe the essence of envy?
2. Do you believe that envy is connected with a person's self-love or self-esteem? Explain.
3. If you were advising someone on how to deal with envy in his or her life, what would be the main points of your advice?
4. From your experience, as a jealous person or as an object of another's jealousy, what do you think are the main ingredients of jealousy?

NOTES

[1]Dolores Curran, "Envy: How Green Are My Values?" *U.S. Catholic,* August 1987, p. 6.

[2]Henry Fairlie, *The Seven Deadly Sins Today,* (Notre Dame: University of Notre Dame Press, 1979), p. 61.

[3]Henry Fairlie, the same, p. 64.

[4]Donald Capps, *Deadly Sins and Saving Virtues,* (Philadelphia: Fortress, 1987), p. 41.

[5]Bernard Häring, *The Law of Christ,* (Westminster, Maryland: Newman Press, 1965), Volume 1, p. 376.

[6]Henry Fairlie, *The Seven Deadly Sins Today,* (Philadelphia: Fortress, 1987), p. 67.

CHAPTER FOUR

Anger

**"The fool gives vent
to all his anger."**

(PROVERBS 29:11)

Meekness

**"Do not let the sun set
on your anger."**

(EPHESIANS 4:26)

I f we could gather a representative group of Catholic men and women who make use of the sacrament of Penance on a regular basis, and if we could get them to tell us what sin they most commonly confess, what would that sin be? It would probably be the sin of anger. We all feel the flame of anger in our hearts. It is a popular passion, a frequent failing.

But if we were to ask these same people to define or describe anger, we might very well draw a blank. We would almost certainly draw a blank if we asked them to tell us why they consider anger a sin. It might be helpful, therefore, if we begin by examining anger first as an emotion (or passion), and secondly as a deadly sin.

ANGER

Anger as an emotion (or passion) is a natural reaction against the narrowing or constricting of our freedom to act as we will or to carry out our desires. It arises when we face obstacles, frustration of our plans, restraint of our activities, insult, or injury.

It is worth underlining this notion that anger flares especially when we run into obstacles, when we cannot have our own way. In daily life this happens often, sometimes in trivial matters, sometimes in important matters. It may happen, for example, when we are delayed by a red light on the way to work in the morning, especially if we are already running late. It may happen when spouses disagree with each other, "No, I do not think we should spend our money on a new TV set." It may happen when the boss tells us we cannot proceed with a pet project.

From these simple examples we can see why anger is such a popular passion. Modern life, for all of its conveniences, seems bent on throwing obstacles into our way! Human relations may almost be described as the art of getting along with others who are trying to thwart us at every step! Delays, frustrations, and disagreements are the daily lot of most people. No wonder anger is a frequent failing!

In addition, unlike some emotions, anger almost always leaves its mark. We know when we are angry. This is so because the emotion of anger is "psychosomatic," that is, it affects us in both our body and soul. Though the bodily changes will be more or less strong depending on the level of our anger, most of us have felt, to some degree or another, the "flush" of anger, the increased pulse, the trembling fingers, the tensed muscles. Anger often brings with it a faster heartbeat, more rapid breathing, tighter stomach muscles. Anger is by no means a passive passion.

The emotion of anger seems to vary according to our basic personality. We sometimes describe people as having a choleric (from choler, which means "wrath") temperament. We consider such people "hot-tempered," easily moved to anger, slow to forget the injury. Sanguine persons, on the other hand, are considered more easygoing, cheerful, optimistic; their anger may flare for a moment but will not last very long.

The emotion of anger is certainly not always a negative one. It can serve many good purposes. Bernard Häring describes the positive value of anger very well: "Well-ordered temper or anger is a tremendous force at man's disposal in the struggle against the obstacles to the good. It is a weapon that can assure victory in the combat against the enemies of virtue, in the struggle for the lofty objectives and ideals which are difficult to attain. If we are incapable of anger, we cannot be dynamic in our love. For if we love the good with all the dynamic force of body and soul, we will oppose evil with equal dynamic force."[1] When we feel anger at instances of cruelty to the elderly, harshness to the poor, meanness to children, this is a positive sign of healthy Christian values.

The stirrings of anger or impatience which many people feel in ordinary daily life are not really sinful. The mother who becomes upset when the baby throws peanut butter at the picture window is not acting sinfully but naturally. There could be sin if she spanked or shook the baby in a vehement and violent way. The man who becomes edgy and agitated during a traffic jam is simply feeling a human emotion. The moral dimension of his anger sets in when he starts cursing at others or driving recklessly to avoid the jam he is in.

Anger as a deadly sin takes on a moral meaning "if," as J.D. Fearon has pointed out, "it leads to vengeful actions that are disproportionate to the injury suffered.…An excessive experience of wrath, the misguided discharge of vengeance, or the objectionable damage done in rage to persons or property could result in sins seriously opposed to justice and charity."[2] The deadly sin of anger shows its face not when we feel the stirrings of emotional agitation but when we willingly desire revenge, damage, destruction.

Anger can be both self-destructive and other-destructive. "It is self-destructive," says Donald Capps, "when it does not reflect a judicious self-restraint, as when it lashes out against the other in blind fury."[3] This is what Saint Thomas means when he says that anger becomes sinful when it is "disordered" or "immoderate"; it is "against reason." It gives more scope to our animal nature than to our rational nature. Such lack of self-restraint or self-discipline in some way dehumanizes angry persons, in some way lessens their dignity.

Anger is also other-destructive. It can destroy not only the other's bodily integrity, as happens in fights and brawls resulting from anger, but also the other's psychic and spiritual integrity. In her comprehensive study of anger, Carol Tavris zeroes in on the moral aspects of anger: "Anger, like love, is a moral emotion. I have watched people use anger, in the name of emotional liberation, to erode affection and trust, whittle away their spirits in bitterness and revenge, diminish their dignity in years of spiteful hatred."[4]

This point needs heavy emphasis. The idea of "ventilating" our anger, of "not stuffing" our angry feelings, is certainly part of modern conventional wisdom. To be sure, this idea has great importance, as we shall see below. But it can also be dangerous. After all, anger is directed at other persons who also have feelings and sensitivities. And anger has consequences which cannot be brushed aside with a weak apology.

In fact the consequences of anger are often bitter and long-lasting. The child who bears the brunt of an angry parent's tongue-lashing may carry the scars for years. The harsh accusations made against a spouse in a fit of anger may destroy the last shreds of love and caring in the heart. Nothing kills the admiration and affection of a friend more quickly than the arrows of unjustified anger.

Dealing With Anger

Personal observations and impressions reveal that people deal with anger in different ways.

There are those persons who regularly give full vent to their anger — "flying off the handle," as we say, moaning and groaning or cursing and swearing. Such behavior resembles that of children who have not yet reached an age when control of emotions can be reasonably expected. Though some psychologists encourage people to "ventilate" their anger and "let off steam," such advice must be carefully understood and prudently practiced. As mentioned above, the recipients of the anger do not usually appreciate it. Throwing a pot at your spouse may make you feel better, but your spouse's head still hurts!

Noticeably, persons who handle anger in this way are largely shunned by others, even by family members and friends. Their behavior causes them to be lonely and isolated. When such immature behavior is chronic, it may well be a symptom of deep emotional disturbance which would profit from professional psychotherapy.

But a large number of people deal with anger in quite another way. They suppress it, refuse to acknowledge it, pretend that it isn't there. They ignore their angry feelings, hoping they will go away. But of course they don't go away. They keep roaming around looking for other ways to rear their ugly heads. These feelings of anger may contribute to brooding, to restlessness, to resentment, even to real depression.

MEEKNESS

Between these two extremes — giving violent vent to anger on the one hand and suppressing it on the other — there is a better way to deal with anger. It is a healthy, constructive, and Christian way. There are four steps to this approach, all of which lead us gradually to the virtue of meekness (patience).

First, *we should allow ourselves to acknowledge our angry feelings and take a good look at them.* Angry feelings, as we have seen, may be positive or negative. When they are positive, we should be grateful for them. When they are negative, we need not be ashamed of them. We can learn from them. We might ask ourselves: "Where are they coming from?" "Why does this or that real or imagined slight arouse such strong feelings in me?" "Is it perhaps that I have made my 'ego' the center of everything and find it constantly thwarted?" Anger often reveals how we feel and think about ourselves, how important we consider our own ideas and opinions. Perhaps we have made ourselves "big shots" and resent any slight against our self-made importance.

In this context, John Garvey makes a very thought-provoking observation: "Consider the occasions on which most of us find ourselves getting angry. Usually they have to do with challenges to our convenience or our authority or our desire to spend a quiet afternoon. Whatever the occasion, anger involves the violation of something we expected. The day did not turn out as we expected it to; and to the degree that our expectation was violated in a major way, not merely rearranged, we explode with varying degrees of vehemence."[5]

Second, *we should allow ourselves to talk about our angry feelings when this is reasonably possible.* It is extremely helpful when family members or coworkers or neighbors can sit down and talk about the causes of the anger that has flared up in their midst. Talking it out is not a panacea for all feelings of anger or for all results of anger, but it can help us focus our anger and begin to seek practical solutions. In family relationships, particularly, it is important to develop the habit of talking about angry feelings, even when they are about rather small and insignificant issues. Then when big issues do arise, the positive pattern will be set.

Peter found that a "family powwow" from time to time came in very handy. Peter and his wife, Charlotte, would gather their four children (two boys, two girls) around the kitchen table. The meeting often started with a prayer. There were strict conditions: no name-calling, no yelling. If one family member had a particular grievance, he or she could speak first. After this presentation, each of the others would have a chance to respond. Peter was often surprised at how many feelings could be expressed and acknowledged and understood in these simple sessions. The whole family agreed that the powwows were worthwhile.

Third, *we should try to learn to contain our anger, not allowing it to overflow its boundaries.* If we do not learn to exercise control, we may find that disagreement with a small decision at work can fester into hatred of the whole company and the entire free-enterprise system of the United States! A snub from a parish priest can provoke us to alienation from the parish community, the pope, even God himself. A teenager arriving home twenty minutes late can occasion an angry parental outburst that damages a parent-child relationship for many months.

Fourth, *we should try to develop the virtues that take the*

wind out of anger, especially meekness, patience, and a sense
of humor. "Meekness moderates anger," says Saint Thomas.
Yet of all the virtues, none is more widely misunderstood than
meekness. "Meekness is not weakness," writes Marilyn Norquist Gustin. "It is a rare and beautiful person who can be
calm, quiet and gentle under attack. He or she is truly inwardly
strong. Meekness springs then not from weakness, but from
the security that makes all violence unnecessary."[6]

Far from being weakness, meekness is rather an inner
strength which enables us to keep things in proper perspective
and helps us to endure injury (real or imagined) without
striking out in return. We should be slow to anger, as the Bible
reminds us. Meekness inspires us to look at the world and the
human condition with compassionate eyes. It teaches us to be
peacemakers by seeing and controlling the aggression and
disorder in our own souls.

"Blessed are the meek;
  for they will inherit the land."

(Matthew 5:5)

Patience — another form of meekness — is also considered
a "sissy" virtue, but only by those who have never tried to
exercise it. Patience is a strong virtue because it inclines us to
suffer and endure present evils without self-pity. It helps us
to face up to the inevitable difficulties and limitations of the
human condition so that they do not overwhelm us with
sadness or prompt us to react to these difficulties and limitations with a growing sense of rage. Patience demands a lot of
fortitude and strength.

A wholesome sense of humor can certainly help us see
what a ridiculous thing anger can be in ourselves and in others.
A sense of humor reminds us to laugh at ourselves rather than

to take ourselves so seriously that we are forever angry at something or someone. There is nothing like a sense of humor to keep things in perspective. To quote John Garvey again: "I look at various items that have known my stupid angers — they range from automobiles that have been thumped on the hood to typewriters that have been throttled (difficult thing, to throttle a typewriter). They all stare back at me, like the rest of the world, mute and unchanged; they are a sign of how little my passions matter."[7]

Pathways to Meekness

With the best will in the world, most of us are still going to yield at times to the deadly sin of anger. Perhaps that's why so many Catholics confess this sin: They are hoping to get a handle on it or to pick up some hints on how to cope with it. The following tips on curbing anger are actually pathways to meekness. They are certainly not original, but they have helped a lot of people.

- Seneca gave very wise advice when he said: "Hesitation is the best cure for anger....The first blows of anger are heavy, but if it waits, it will think again." This advice was made practical by Thomas Jefferson: "When angry, count to ten before you speak; if very angry, a hundred."
- Saint Paul shows his understanding of human nature when he admonishes: "Do not let the sun set on your anger, and do not leave room for the devil" (Ephesians 4:26-27). Anger has a way of festering in the soul; the longer it festers, the more ugly it gets. The sooner the infection of anger can be excised, the better.
- In his teaching about anger, Jesus places heavy emphasis on the spirit of reconciliation. It is one of the most urgent demands of discipleship. "If you bring your gift to the altar,

and there recall that your brother has anything against you, leave your gift there at the altar, go first and be reconciled with your brother, and then come and offer your gift" (Matthew 5:23-24). Besides being a demand of discipleship, this openness to reconciliation can in a surprising way provide gentle healing for our angry souls.

Reflection/Discussion Questions

1. From your own experience, can you give an example of "well-ordered or just anger"? Explain in some detail.
2. Give your opinion of this statement: "Once thought to be a destructive emotion that should be suppressed at all costs, anger is now widely thought to be a healthy emotion that costs too much when it is suppressed."
3. If you were to describe a meek person, what characteristics would you highlight?
4. Do you think that "counting to ten" really helps you in dealing with anger?

NOTES

[1]Bernard Häring, *The Law of Christ*, (Westminster, Maryland: Newman Press, 1965) Volume 1, p. 337.

[2]J.D. Fearon, "Anger," *New Catholic Encyclopedia*.

[3]Donald Capps, *Deadly Sins and Saving Virtues*, (Philadelphia: Fortress, 1987), p. 83.

[4]Carol Tavris, *Anger: The Misunderstood Emotion*, (New York: Simon and Shuster, 1982), p. 40.

[5]John Garvey, "Anger," *U.S. Catholic*, August 1987, p. 14.

[6]Marilyn Norquist Gustin, *Jesus' Pattern for a Happy Life: The Beatitudes*, (Liguori, MO: Liguori Publications, 1981), p. 40.

[7]John Garvey, article cited, p. 15.

CHAPTER FIVE

Sloth

"Like a moth in clothing... sorrow gnaws at the human heart."
(PROVERBS 25:20)

Joy

"Your grief will become joy."
(JOHN 16:20)

H is name was Bill. His friends called him "Big Bill," and with good reason. He was six feet four inches tall and weighed about two hundred twenty-five pounds. At forty-seven he was still in good physical shape — but not in such good spiritual shape.

"I've had it with the Church," said Bill. "Or maybe it would be more honest to say I've had it with God. In the late sixties I was really turned on. My wife and I made a Marriage Encounter. Our family started praying together, I became active in youth work, I was a member of the peace and justice committee in our parish. I felt good about helping to build a new world. But now I feel disillusioned, empty. It all seems like a pious dream. I don't see any change in the world. I feel like giving up...."

What is Big Bill's problem? It is certainly possible that he is suffering from burnout. It's a common ailment these days — a feeling of disinterest, a lack of caring, a turning away from responsibility, a withdrawal from social commitments. If allowed to continue, it can become quite serious. "When the term is used with some legitimacy," writes William Flaherty, "burnout goes beyond being simply tired and fed up or needing time off. It is a psychological condition that needs therapy."[1]

SLOTH

It is quite possible that Big Bill is suffering from the deadly sin of sloth. Of all the deadly sins, this one has the most misleading name. When we think of sloth, we naturally think of old-fashioned laziness, of not wanting to be inconvenienced, not wanting to exert ourselves over things we'd rather not do. We think, for example, of the man who avoids mowing the lawn because he wants to watch his favorite team on TV; or the woman who wants to get away from the daily demands by soaking up the sun's rays for a few hours.

Is this what we mean by the deadly sin of sloth? No, this is not what sloth is all about. In this hectic world, such examples of "sloth" might actually be considered virtues! Certainly many people who live in the fast lane could profit from more leisure moments: time to walk with a child or read a book or tinker with an old car. Such leisure time is certainly not a sign of sloth.

Since the English word *sloth* is used in so many different ways, it is helpful to give this deadly sin a more accurate name. That name is *acedia,* a Greek word meaning "not caring" or "apathy." But it is not just apathy in general; it is apathy of the spirit.

Saint Thomas defines this sin of sloth as "sorrow for spiritual good" or, more fully, as "an oppressive sorrow which so weighs on a person's mind that he or she wants to do nothing about spiritual goods." Bernard Häring describes sloth as "a lack of zeal for things spiritual" or "a lack of spirit in opposing the heavy pull and pressure of earthly things and rising to the level of the divine."[2]

From a slightly different viewpoint, Henry Fairlie defines sloth as "a state of dejection that gives rise to torpor of mind and feeling and spirit; to a sluggishness or, as it has been put, a poisoning of the will; to despair, faintheartedness, and even desirelessness, a lack of real desire for anything, even for what is good."[3]

Whatever particular definition we settle on, we see that the deadly sin of sloth has elements of apathy about spiritual things, indifference toward spiritual responsibilities, listlessness in doing good. Sloth almost always brings with it a large dose of self-pity. At the same time it drives joy out of the human heart.

Granted that these descriptions give us a clearer picture of the deadly sin with the misleading name, how does this sin actually touch our lives today? Without too much effort we can think of a number of ways.

Sloth and Spiritual Responsibilities

It is clear that many people are unfaithful to their spiritual and religious responsibilities precisely because of the difficulties involved. Luke and Kim were a young couple who came to the rectory to make arrangements for marriage in the Catholic Church. In response to a set number of questions I asked them, it became clear that, though they wanted to be married in the Catholic Church, they were certainly not by any stretch of the imagination "practicing Catholics."

I asked them how often they attended Sunday Mass where the Catholic community gathers around the altar to give praise and thanksgiving to God in and with Jesus Christ. They told me they seldom attended Mass. I asked them how often they prayed in the course of an average week. They said they seldom prayed. I asked them if they were involved in any small way with sharing their faith with others. They said that they never thought about it.

This scenario may not be all that exceptional in our day, but it is worthwhile examining the reasons given for not being faithful to even these minimal practices of faith. Luke said he couldn't get to Mass on Sundays because that was the only day he had to sleep, and he was so tired because he worked hard all week. Kim said that she was always running late, so she didn't have time for prayer in the morning, and she was dead tired at night and couldn't pray then either. They didn't feel that they had enough time or energy to share with anybody else; it was hard enough just to take care of themselves.

Luke and Kim were guilty of sloth in the classical meaning of the term. The early Christians used to say that "true devotion" was the opposite of sloth and the cure for it. True devotion is the inner will to give ourselves wholeheartedly to things concerning the worship and service of God, even when these things are difficult, even when we are tired or busy or rushed. Obviously, this is the opposite of sloth, because sloth says: I will give myself to the worship and service of God when it is convenient, when I'm not tired, when I'm not busy, when there's nothing else to do....

Unfortunately, there are a lot of Catholics like Luke and Kim. It is not just that they do not practice their Catholic faith but rather that they hide behind such weak excuses for not doing so. The real reasons are that they have lost their esteem and love for the things of God because they have found them difficult. Because of their many excuses, however, they never face this fact. They may not even be aware that the spirit is dying in them. What they really need is a dose of "true devotion" to offset the poison of sloth.

Sloth and Social Justice

If sloth pushes us to neglect "the city of God," it also pushes us to neglect "the city of man." The deadly sin of sloth consists not only in apathy toward spiritual realities but also indifference, and even coldness, to the needs of society. "Sloth is preeminently a sin of omission. To put it more positively, it is a sin of neglect. We neglect what we ought to do, and especially we neglect our neighbors."[4]

At a time when technology has taken much of the drudgery out of our work, at a time when many people have more education and leisure than ever before, what is happening? Certainly not what should be happening. Each year the number of citizens who take the time and trouble to vote keeps decreasing. Almost every charitable organization dedicated to service for the poor and needy reports that volunteers grow fewer every year. Many Christian service commissions in parishes around the country keep going because of a few dedicated people, while the majority go their own way.

As with spiritual responsibilities, so with social action for justice and charity; we tend to make excuses. As members of the richest nation on the face of the earth, we do not seem to mind that there are hungry children and homeless families, not only in foreign lands but even in our own communities. Instead of turning outward, we turn inward upon ourselves, having become firmly convinced that we have to look out for number one.

Where does this apathy come from? Psychiatrist Karl

Menninger gives several clues. "In some individuals it can be an egocentricity...born of fearfulness and uncertainty, or a lack of imagination. It appears as a 'don't care' attitude which no amount of sentimentalizing as 'contentedness,' 'minding one's own business,' and 'living and letting live' can cover up. A common excuse for inaction, indifference, or lukewarm response is the 'fear of becoming involved.' Exactly, yet all life is a matter of involvement somewhere with something, many somethings, and this chronic fear and consequent withdrawal is surely a common sin."[5]

Pope John XXIII was quoted as saying that the purpose of religion is to comfort the afflicted and to afflict the comfortable. To be sure, there are many afflicted people in our society who need much comfort. Unfortunately, there are also many people who need to be roused from their comfort and their sloth. The Lord God, speaking through the prophet Isaiah, would not let pious people get away with the religious act of fasting, while at the same time ignoring their brothers and sisters. The Word of the Lord, calling us to social justice, should shake us loose from the deadly sin of sloth:

Do you call this a fast,
    a day acceptable to the LORD?
This, rather, is the fasting that I wish:
    releasing those bound unjustly,
    untying the thongs of the yoke;
Setting free the oppressed,
    breaking every yoke;
Sharing your bread with the hungry,
    sheltering the oppressed and the homeless;
Clothing the naked when you see them,
    and not turning your back on your own.

                                        (Isaiah 58:5-7)

Sloth and Self-pity

Saint Gregory the Great, who wrote so much about the capital sins, liked to describe the main sin as "the parent" and sins related to the main sin as "the children." Thus some of the "children" of sloth are rancor, melancholy, malaise, despair. In an insightful article on sloth, William Flaherty makes an interesting remark: "One sin is not mentioned in the genealogies, but certainly one of the children of acedia is indulged self-pity."[6] This certainly seems to be true.

What is self-pity? It is a habit of concentrating on the daily troubles and sorrows we all experience. It is a grim determination to look only at the gloomy side of life. It is a pattern of refusing to think about the beautiful and joyful realities of our lives, such as the loveliness of nature, the faithfulness of friends, the comfort of good health. It often includes an habitual resentment of others who are held responsible for our troubles and afflictions.

The dragon of self-pity does not necessarily snort a lot. Sometimes it sneaks up on us in a quiet way. A good way to know if the dragon is making a move on us is to monitor the questions we ask ourselves: "Why don't my children appreciate all the work I do around this house?" "Why am I the only one who ever puts gas in the car?" "Why does the boss always blame me when things go wrong?" "Why doesn't my spouse show a little understanding once in a while?" "Why do my friends call me only when they need something?"

It is not certain, but it is very probable that these questions are self-pity questions. Most of them are about small things, but small things have a way of becoming large and of dominating our lives. These questions have a "moaning and groaning" sound to them. That is almost always a tip-off that the dragon is doing his thing with us.

It has been said that "a little self-pity never hurt anybody." That may be true, but a little self-pity can easily become a lot of self-pity, and that can hurt us in many ways. Self-pity tends to eat away at our relationships with other people. It has a way of casting a black shadow over our judgment of others, especially those with whom we live and work. It easily enlarges itself, so that what started out as feeling blue about some small problem all of a sudden colors our entire perspective of life.

Speaking of self-pity, William Flaherty makes some wise observations and ends up with a good question: "Americans may be tired of banal exhortations to make no small plans, to dream big dreams, and to meet the glorious challenges of tomorrow head-on....But today's 'hard times' give Christians little justification for prolonged spiritual wound-licking. Who sewed up the eyelids of our faith if we can't see the daily miracles of beauty and joy around us?"[7]

JOY

Many theologians have contrasted the deadly sin of sloth with the life-giving virtue of fortitude. Sloth denotes weakness in time of adversity; fortitude denotes courage in the face of trials. There are, to be sure, trials and adversities and suffering in every person's life. But we must learn to face them with courage and accept them with joy.

Like pebbles on a beach, suffering is part of the human landscape. And, like pebbles, suffering comes in different shapes and sizes. Our crosses may be internal or external; they may be physical, psychological, spiritual. We are all familiar with the catalog of human suffering: the loss of health, financial worries, emotional upheavals, the breakdown of relationships with family or friends, disillusionment like that of Big Bill, loneliness, depression…and so many more as well.

The key question that confronts us is not whether we will suffer but how we will suffer. Throughout history people have sought a solution to suffering. There are many philosophies and theologies. Buddhism, for example, taught that the best approach is to suppress all desire and thus experience nirvana or oblivion. If we desire nothing, we cannot be hurt or disappointed. The Stoic school of philosophy stressed an attitude of endurance in the face of pain, a refusal to acknowledge suffering or give into complaint.

The Christian view, in most simple terms, is courageous, even joyful, acceptance of suffering in union with Christ. His sufferings were redemptive, life-giving, because they were enriched with love. If our sufferings are united with the sufferings of Christ, if they are motivated by love, they too can be redemptive. The deadly sin of sloth will tempt us to an attitude of bitterness, hardheartedness, coldness in the face of suffering. Slothful persons show pain and grief at being called to the follow Christ. Courageous Christians do their best to respond lovingly to the mandate of Jesus: "If anyone wishes to come after me, he must deny himself and take up his cross daily and follow me" (Luke 9:23).

Obviously, there is an intimate connection between sloth seen as apathy toward spiritual responsibilities and social justice. It is even more evident in our battle with self-pity. The latter fault definitely takes away our joy. For this reason, Saint Thomas reminds us that sloth is "opposed to the joy of charity." Sometimes we forget how often the Scriptures speak of joy. Joy is an integral part of the gospels. After commanding his followers to live in love, Jesus says: "I have told you this so that my joy might be in you and your joy might be complete" (John 15:11). A little later in the Gospel of John, after informing his disciples that he would be leaving this world and promising them that he would send the Holy Spirit upon them, Jesus states: "I say to you, you will weep and mourn, while the world rejoices; you will grieve, but your grief will become joy" (John 16:20).

Saint Paul affirms that joy should be central to the Christian's attitude and also underlines the reason why. "Rejoice in the Lord always. I shall say it again: rejoice! Your kindness should be known to all. The Lord is near" (Philippians 4:4-5). Our joy is rooted in the reality of the Lord's presence, in his gift of the Spirit to us. Because he is near, because his gentle love envelopes us, joy — even amid the anxiety and turmoil of life — should be ours.

Joy is a deep feeling of happiness based on the actual attainment of something valuable or on the secure promise of its attainment. As Christians, we have a lot to be joyful about! We are sure that God's love for us is freely given, unconditional, and changeless. We already possess it! Moreover, God, who is faithful to his promises, has promised us his help and grace in time of trials and difficulties. Though sloth makes us fear our spiritual responsibilities, Jesus assures us that his yoke is easy and his burden light. God wants us to be joyful people, not apathetic and indifferent and sour. The goodness of God is all around us; he is indeed the cause of our joy. In him, as Jesus promised, our joy will be complete.

Reflection/Discussion Questions

1. Do you think the English word *sloth* conveys the basic idea of this deadly sin? If not, what English word would you use instead?
2. Polls say that many Catholics, as much as half, do not regularly practice their religion. Do you think this is mainly due to sloth or to other causes?

3. Among your relatives and friends, do you find a reluctance to volunteer for community projects? If so, what do you think are the reasons?
4. Do you agree that the virtue which opposes sloth is joy? If not, with what virtue would you replace it?

NOTES

[1]William Flaherty, "Sloth: Fools Rush In," *U.S. Catholic*, August 1987, p. 9.

[2]Bernard Häring, *The Law of Christ,* (Westminster, Maryland: Newman Press, 1965), Volume 1, p. 381.

[3]Henry Fairlie, *The Seven Capital Sins Today,* (Notre Dame: University of Notre Dame Press, 1979) p. 113.

[4]Henry Fairlie, the same, p. 129.

[5]Karl Menninger, *Whatever Became of Sin?* (New York: E.P. Dutton Publishers, 1973) hardcover, p. 146.

[6]William Flaherty, article cited, p. 9.

[7]William Flaherty, article cited, p. 9-10.

CHAPTER SIX

Avarice

"You cannot serve God and mammon."

(MATTHEW 6:24)

Poverty

**"For where your treasure is,
there also will your heart be."**

(MATTHEW 6:21)

O ne of the first points to decide about the deadly sin of avarice is what to name it. Some call it covetousness; others call it greed. In ordinary language we use these various words indiscriminately. Some experts say that there is a shade of difference among them. *Webster's Seventh New College Dictionary,* for example, says that the covetous are "marked by inordinate desire for wealth or possessions or for another's possessions." The word *greedy* "stresses lack of restraint and often of discrimination in desire." Avaricious, in its turn, "implies obsessive acquisitiveness especially of money and strongly suggests stinginess."

AVARICE

Whatever English word is chosen, the basic idea of this deadly sin is fairly clear. A sampling of theological definitions makes this evident. Saint Thomas defines avarice as "immoderate love of possessing." Bernard Häring writes that "avarice is inordinate pursuit of material values."[1] Patrick Meager points out that avarice consists "in excessive appetite for wealth."[2]

Like all the deadly sins, avarice implies a lack of moderation or balance in regard to something — money, wealth — that is not evil in itself but is capable of corrupting the human heart, of diverting the human person from other more important values, and even of leading to sins against justice and charity.

There are, of course, degrees of avarice and greed. The highest degree consists of seeing material goods as the ultimate end of human existence. That is why Saint Paul refers to it as "idolatry" and states that the greedy will not inherit the kingdom of God (see Ephesians 5:5). There are many lesser degrees as well: for example, seeking our self-esteem from the possessions we own; allowing wealth and possessions to distract us from spiritual things; placing material goods before people and the needs of people in our lives.

Malice of Avarice

Why is avarice a deadly sin? Because it is the fountainhead of many false values and evil actions.

First of all, it can so easily erode our spiritual instincts and in a sense make us less than human. "Greed is deadly because it distracts us from what is important in life....It distorts our vision and gives us a false perception of ourselves and the world."[3] Greed rouses our vicious instincts; it repels us from growing as human beings. "We depersonalize our own selves in our avarice, in the objects that we use to represent and announce our status, and in the end we dehumanize ourselves....Avarice leads to a form of self-annihilation."[4]

Second, because avarice catches us up in the pursuit of "more" for its own sake, it distracts us from caring about those who have practically nothing. Avarice places a blindfold over our eyes so that we no longer see the poor and needy among us. Saint Thomas tells us that greed takes mercy from our hearts and makes us unfeeling toward others. The avaricious will not give a dollar to the poor because they always fear that they may not have quite enough for themselves.

Third, avarice is often a driving force to immoral acts, such as stealing, bribery, embezzlement, and all forms of "white-collar" crime. Once the desire to "possess," to "own," to "acquire," is given free reign in our hearts, the temptation to fulfill this desire by any means is very deep and strong. For this reason, no doubt, Yahweh delivered one of his commandments in this form: "You shall not covet your neighbor's house. You shall not covet your neighbor's wife, nor his male or female slave, nor his ox or ass, nor anything that belongs to him" (Exodus 20:17). Yahweh spoke often about covetousness (see, for example, Deuteronomy 7:25 and Micah 2:2) and roundly condemned the coveter for social injustice.

Faces of Avarice

Are modern American men and women more avaricious than their ancestors? Or are they simply more severely tempted because of the high standard of living our culture offers and because of the insistent power of advertising?

It has been said that in every society, even a professedly classless one like ours, there are various groupings. There are the "old rich" who take wealth for granted, are not particularly ostentatious about it, and may even be tempted to share a bit of it. There are the "new rich" who are carried away by wealth and dedicate their lives to conspicuous consumption. Of course, there are always the poor who have no material possessions to be greedy about.

What about the middle class? In our society perhaps the middle class are the most avaricious of all. The desire to keep on climbing up the ladder of success can easily dominate their lives. Do we not see this all around us? The clothes, the car, the furniture, the home, are never quite good enough. Nothing is ever quite enough. Yet they are so often the people who "cannot afford" another child, who "cannot afford" to contribute to charities.

Sadder still is the way so many people are sacrificing their health, their marriages, their peace of mind, just to get a "little more." Constantly, we hear that both spouses must work outside the home "in order to make ends meet." But how did the ends get so far apart? True, much of this is due to the high cost of living in today's world. But some of it must be partly due to greed.

Greed "implies an insatiable desire to possess or acquire something in an amount far greater than we need."[5] How much do we really need? Isn't the observation of Henry Fairlie at least partly true: "We buy more clothes than we need, more accessories (how revealing the word is) than we need, more furniture than we need, more bric-a-brac than we need, more *objects d'art* than we need, more cookbooks than we need, more kitchen equipment than we need, and even more gifts for our friends than they need."[6]

Teaching of Jesus

Considering the deep drives of our unredeemed nature for possession and ownership, admitting the materialistic and consumer-oriented aspects of our culture, what are we as Christians to do? We must take another look at the teaching of Jesus on material possessions.

Money plays an important part in everybody's life. There is no escape from the need for some material possessions in human life. And even beyond the necessities of food and shelter and clothing, there seems to be a deep yen in most people, as we have seen, for material things.

Knowing human nature as he did, Jesus often addressed himself to the basic questions of material goods and our attitudes toward them. It is difficult, however, to formulate a balanced view of the teaching of Jesus on material goods. We run the risk of watering down some of his very hard sayings. We also run the risk of reading into the Scriptures our own pet ideas. But maybe we can stand back and take an honest look at what the gospels say to us.[7]

In the first place, Jesus did not condemn out of hand the possession and use of material things. In the famous passage about the birds of the air and the lilies of the field, Jesus quite directly acknowledges, "Your heavenly Father knows that you need them all" (Matthew 6:32). The urgent concern of Jesus was with the attitude of people toward material goods. There is a danger that we can make them the be-all and end-all of our lives. Remember that "where your treasure is, there also will your heart be" (Matthew 6:21). We can become slaves to money and all that money can buy. "No one can serve two masters....You cannot serve God and mammon" (Matthew 6:24). As is so often true in the preaching of Jesus, it is the heart that matters!

In popular Jewish belief at the time of Jesus, wealth was often considered a sign of God's favor. Those who were good and righteous God would reward with wealth. Jesus exploded this myth. "It will be hard for one who is rich to enter the kingdom of heaven....It is easier for a camel to pass through the eye of a needle than for one who is rich to enter the kingdom of God" (Matthew 19:23-24).

Once again, the problem seems to be not so much about money in itself but the illusion that somehow money makes a person morally good or independent of God and others. "Take care to guard against all greed, for though one may be rich, one's life does not consist of possessions" (Luke 12:15). The rich farmer who was so smug about his wealth and so self-centered about its use would hear God say: "You fool, this night your life will be demanded of you; and the things you have prepared, to whom will they belong?" (Luke 12:20). On this Jesus comments: "Thus will it be for the one who stores up treasure for himself but is not rich in what matters to God" (Luke 12:21).

It is hard for the rich to enter the kingdom of God, but not impossible. The disciples (in the story of the rich young man) were aware that many of their contemporaries considered wealth a sign of God's favor. When Jesus denied this assumption, they concluded that practically no one could be saved. Jesus replied that it was possible for the rich to be saved if they, like the poor, recognized their dependence on God for their salvation (see Matthew 19:16-26).

On balance, then, the teaching of Jesus seems to be concerned not so much with the good or bad of material things but with the attitudes, the values, and the priorities of those who wish to follow him. The true disciple must know that it is not money that makes the world go round but freedom, trust, and ultimately, love.

POVERTY

Very early in the life of the Church some men and women decided to take the story of the rich young man at face value. In that story a young man asks Jesus what he must do to gain eternal life. Jesus tells him to keep the commandments and names them. The young man replies: " 'All of these I have observed. What do I still lack?' Jesus said to him, 'If you wish to be perfect, go, sell what you have and give to [the] poor, and you will have treasure in heaven. Then come, follow me' " (Matthew 19:20-21). Those early Christians embraced what came to be called "evangelical (or gospel) poverty."

In the course of time, as religious communities of men and women became more structured under the authority of the Church, the vow or counsel of poverty came into existence. This vow entailed certain norms (sometimes quite complex) about the ownership and independent use of material goods. While there have been variations on this vow of poverty in the history of the Church, the basic idea of this vow and counsel has been fairly constant over the years. The present law of the Church describes it this way: "The evangelical counsel of poverty in imitation of Christ who, although He was rich became poor for us, entails, besides a life which is poor in fact and in spirit, a life of labor lived in moderation and foreign to earthly riches, a dependence and a limitation in the use and disposition of goods according to the norm of the proper law of each institute" (*Code of Canon Law,* #600).

It goes without saying that religious communities, in the course of time, have been more or less fervent in their observance of this counsel. There have been periods of faithful observance, giving great witness to the whole Church, and periods of extreme laxity, giving scandal to many. In our time the observance seems to be in a state of confusion and the witness value seems thin, as it is not uncommon to hear laypeople say to a religious: "You take the vow of poverty, but we keep it." Like the Church itself, religious communities are in need of continual reformation.

But the virtue of gospel or evangelical poverty is by no means the private preserve of religious communities. It applies to all disciples of Jesus, whatever their state in life or actual living conditions. What is meant by evangelical poverty? Like so many rich Christian concepts, it is hard to define in clear-cut terms. But one of the best descriptions was written by Pope Paul VI in 1971.[8] He urges us in no uncertain terms to listen to the cry of the poor.

Cry of the Poor

To overcome our tendency to avarice we must learn to listen to the cry of the poor. "You hear rising up, more pressing than ever, from their personal stress and collective misery, 'the cry of the poor.' " It is a cry that arose not only in biblical times, not only in times of primitive technology, but one that arises even in our affluent age. "In a world experiencing the full flood of development this persistence of poverty-stricken masses and individuals still constitutes a pressing call."

"How will this cry of the poor," asks the Pope, "find an echo in your lives?" He answers this question by providing several guidelines.

First, the cry of the poor must bar us "from whatever would be a compromise with any form of social injustice." From hard experience we know that social injustice is all around us, and we know how easy it is to compromise with it! Among other things, social injustice certainly includes dishonest business practices, disregard for the rights of employees or employers, neglectful and even harsh treatment of the truly needy. Who among us has not compromised with these injustices?

Second, the cry of the poor must keep us from being "carried away by an uncurbed seeking of our own ease" and from being "enticed by the security of possessions, knowledge and power."

Third, the cry of the poor must encourage us to "fraternal sharing with our needy brothers and sisters. Such sharing is an imperative of evangelical poverty. It is a sharing that calls for generosity and trust in the Lord. It is related to what Michael Foley has called "the poverty of enough." The truth is that many of us have enough and more than enough. But we are afraid to say "enough."

Option for the Poor

One of the most important religious events of 1986 was the publication of the U.S. Bishops' *Economic Justice for All: Pastoral Letter on Catholic Social Teaching and the U.S. Economy*. This far-ranging letter is beyond the scope of this booklet. But in considering the deadly sin of avarice, there is one point of the letter that should be underlined. It is called the preferential option for the poor.

The bishops explain the purpose of this preferential option for the poor: "The obligation to evaluate social and economic activity from the viewpoint of the poor and the powerless arises from the radical command to love one's neighbor as one's self. Those who are marginalized and whose rights are denied have privileged claims if society is to provide justice for *all*."[9]

This option for the poor is not meant to pit one group or class against another. Rather, it recognizes that the deprivation and powerlessness of the poor wounds the whole community. "These wounds will be healed only by greater solidarity with the poor and among the poor themselves."[10]

It is fashionable in some circles for affluent people to speak romantically about the poor. Such talk can make affluent people feel good, but it doesn't help the poor very much! The bishops avoid such idle talk. They believe that the preferential option for the poor demands several urgent priorities for our nation and several for us as individual Christians.

In regard to national goals, the fulfillment of the basic needs of the poor is the first priority. Meeting human needs, such as nutrition, housing, education, and health, must come before the fulfillment of desires for luxury consumer goods, excessive profits, and unnecessary military hardware.

A second priority should also be placed on policies that would give those who are now excluded from the economic mainstream a chance to participate actively in the nation's economic life. More is required than a handout. Needed are policies and programs that will help people help themselves in a meaningful way.

A third priority "presents a strong moral challenge to policies that put large amounts of talent and capital into the production of luxury consumer goods and military technology while failing to invest sufficiently in education, health, the basic infrastructure of our society, and economic sectors that produce urgently needed jobs, goods, and services."[11]

On this level of national priorities, there is the temptation for us individual Christians to think that "they" (the government, politicians) should do it. But what about our personal responsibilities? We might use several questions to examine our personal attitudes.

- In this consumer society, how can I develop a healthy detachment from material goods and avoid the temptation to assess who I am by what I have?
- How will my economic choices to buy, sell, invest, hire, and fire serve human dignity and the common good?
- Are there some practical ways that I can share my time, my talent, and my treasure with those in need?

Reflection/Discussion Questions

1. In the text of this chapter, several points are developed under "malice of avarice." Do you agree with these? Do any others come to mind?

2. Is it fair or unfair to say that in the U.S. at this time the middle class is most caught up in avarice or greed?
3. Do you think Pope Paul VI's explanation of gospel poverty has much relevance for modern Catholics? Explain your answer.
4. Share your thoughts and feelings on the three questions posed in the text at the end of this chapter.

NOTES

[1]Bernard Häring, *The Law of Christ,* (Westminster, Maryland, Newman Press, 1965), Volume 1, p. 378.

[2]Patrick Meager, "Avarice," *New Catholic Encyclopedia.*

[3]Donald Capps, *Deadly Sins and Saving Virtues,* (Philadelphia: Fortress Press, 1987), p. 36.

[4]Henry Fairlie, *The Seven Deadly Sins Today,* (Notre Dame: University of Notre Dame Press, 1979), p. 140.

[5]Capps, in the work cited, p. 35.

[6]Fairlie, in the work cited, p. 136.

[7]For more on the teaching of Jesus, see Daniel L. Lowery, *The Parables of Jesus,* (Liguori, MO: Liguori Publications, 1987), chapter 5.

[8]Pope Paul VI, "Evangelical Witness," in Austin Flannery (Editor), *Vatican Council II: The Conciliar and Post Conciliar Documents,* p. 680 ff.

[9]*Economic Justice for All: Pastoral Letter on Catholic Social Teaching and the U.S. Economy,* (Washington, DC: National Conference of Catholic Bishops, 1986) #87.

[10]*EJFA,* #88.

[11]*EJFA,* #92.

CHAPTER SEVEN

Gluttony

"Their God is their stomach."

(PHILIPPIANS 3:19)

Temperance

"In whatever you do, be moderate."

(SIRACH 31:22)

One of the ugliest characteristics of affluent people is that they take so many things for granted. Eileen, a middle-aged woman, decided several years ago to start a catering company. Her reputation is so good that she caters many of the large business and civic dinners in the city. In response to the question: "How's business, Eileen?" she gave an impassioned reply. "Business is good, but some things about catering really tick me off. I grew up during the Depression; we had enough to eat but were taught never to waste food. The well-off people I work for could care less about wasting food. Most of my friends don't give a second thought to the food that is wasted in their homes. They worry about when they will eat and where they will eat and what they will eat, but they just take the food for granted."

For many of us Christians, "taking the food for granted"

may be our sin of gluttony. As long as we have enough money to pay for the groceries, we go our merry way. Like the rich man in the well-known parable of Jesus, we eat well every day but do not seem to be very concerned about the Lazaruses who go to bed hungry every night (see Luke 16:19-31). Dennis McBride catches the heart of this parable when he writes: "The rich man did not assault or abuse Lazarus: He did nothing and that was his crime. He treated Lazarus as if he were already dead; he forgot about Lazarus; and Lazarus died of his forgetfulness. It was the rich man's apathy, his insensitivity, which proved ground enough for his damnation."[1]

Nor do we give much thought to a simpler lifestyle that might, in some small way, help the poor and hungry. We do not seem to hear the call of the American bishops to take a stand on the burning issues of farm and food policy in the United States.[2]

GLUTTONY

Given this tendency to take food (and drink) for granted, it is easy to see that the word *gluttony* implies excess. In its basic meaning it signifies excess in eating or drinking. But we also use it in a metaphorical sense, as when we say someone is a "glutton for punishment" or a "glutton for work." As we think about our lives in the last decade of the twentieth century, it may be that the word "excess" most aptly describes us. Are not many people today dealing with excesses in eating, drinking, doping, smoking, working, playing? In recent years we have even coined new words. In addition to alcoholic, we now have foodaholic, workaholic…. Where will it all end?

Obviously, we cannot touch on all of these excesses in this chapter. But in the context of the deadly sin of gluttony and the life-giving virtue of temperance (moderation), it might be helpful for us to consider the excesses that afflict so many lives: namely, excesses in regard to food, alcohol, other drugs.

Food Consumption

In the Scriptures food is considered a good thing, a blessing from a provident God. Food is necessary for sustaining life; it gives pleasure and refreshment to the human person; it provides an opportunity for "table fellowship," sharing our food with others in a friendly atmosphere. The Book of Sirach teaches that "gluttony is evil," but moderate eating is good for the body and mind. The advice of the wise man is: "In whatever you do, be moderate..." (Sirach 31:22).

Saint Thomas Aquinas further refined this idea of moderation. He defines the deadly sin of gluttony as "an inordinate desire of eating and drinking." That word "inordinate," which Saint Thomas applies to almost all the deadly sins, is another word for excessive, unregulated, intemperate, or immoderate. Saint Paul gives an extreme example of inordinate desire for food when he describes those for whom "their God is their stomach" (Philippians 3:19). But the Christian tradition goes out of its way to insist that the normal desire for food, far from being sinful, is natural and necessary and healthy. It is the excessive or inordinate desire for food that constitutes the deadly sin of gluttony.

When we consider gluttony in our modern American society, it is this dimension of excess or lack of moderation that stands out. The modern sin of gluttony is a kind of obsession with food, not for its own sake but for its symbolic value: to reduce boredom, to give meaning to life, to make up for disappointments, to ease guilt and anxiety. Kenneth Guentert writes about it in this way: "Does gluttony exist in a culture where the national food is the potato chip and the national body type a pencil? Yes, gluttony exists. And it has everything to do with obsession. People don't always have the rotund bodies to show for it, but the anorexic, the bulemic, the gourmet, and the chronic dieter are all obsessed with food. They're all gluttons in their own way."[3]

Responsible Care of Health

A Christian moral principle that guards us against gluttony concerns the proper care of our health. It may be stated thus: As human persons we have a moral responsibility to take reasonable care of our health. "Health" here is understood in the "holistic" sense: the care of and harmony between our physical, mental, emotional, and spiritual capacities. Obviously, it is impossible to give an exact list of all that is demanded by this moral principle, but it includes our responsibility to maintain a balanced diet, take adequate exercise, achieve a proper blend of work and rest and recreation, and other such reasonable steps.

In light of this Christian principle, the question arises as to whether the widespread preoccupations with food and weight and body image are not unbalanced, out of all proportion. "Health spas" have sprung up throughout the land in order to help men and women who eat too much, or too much of the wrong foods, to lose weight. Chances are that some of these men and women are represented in the study done by a large national food company. The study concluded that millions of Americans think about food for at least three hours a day, not including the time actually spent in eating! Perhaps no society in history has been as food conscious and as weight conscious as ours. "Thin is in, but fat is where it's at!"

Concern for sensible dieting and regular exercise is certainly important. But the preoccupation with weight and body shape seems to bring almost a pagan dimension to life. After all, there can be a cult of bodily care which attaches excessive importance to physical health and body image. What seems to be lacking in the whole picture is a wholesome sense of Christian responsibility and a positive regard for moderation.

Food Sickness

Moderation is especially lacking in the compulsive eating disorders about which we hear so much these days. Bulimia, the urge to splurge on food and then to purge oneself of it, is a crippling obsession for a number of people, notably young women. Anorexia, the loss or suppression of appetite over an extended period of time, results often enough in severe weight loss, physical weakness, and severe medical problems.

Mary Ann is a young woman in her early twenties. Her black hair and dark-brown eyes are naturally attractive, but she does not look attractive. She looks emaciated, tired, sad. She has just finished a counseling session concerning her problem of bulimia. She is pleased with the way the counseling is going. "I'm beginning to understand," she says, "that the problem is not really about food or vomiting. The problem is how I see myself: I have never loved myself or felt loved. I have been racked with guilt that I caused my parents' divorce when I was eight years old. I know it sounds silly. In counseling I'm finally getting to know myself and my feelings. I'm beginning to understand my compulsions."

To be sure, these eating disorders are not so much about food as they are about self-image, love, and relationships. We are talking here not about sin but about sickness. The sickness is not primarily of the body but of the psyche and the soul. The disorders are rooted in the personality, expressed through the manner of eating or not eating. These disorders are serious and progressive illnesses. They need professional intervention.

Fortunately, in more and more places there are treatment centers for those who suffer from these eating disorders. One doctor who specializes in treatment of these disorders offers hope by pointing out that bulimia and anorexia, even in their most chronic and progressively deteriorating stages, have a high incidence of recovery if properly treated. Blessed are they who, like Mary Ann, acknowledge their need for help and find the help they need.

Alcohol Usage

The use of alcohol is widespread in our society. Its prevalence in all kinds of social situations is partly due, no doubt, to our general level of affluence. Certainly, many people have come to believe that alcohol is necessary for a good time. When we speak about the "war on drugs," we perhaps do not advert to the fact that alcohol is itself a powerful drug and, because it is legal, more widely used than other drugs. Taken in sufficient quantity, this drug has serious effects on the body and the mind.

Many religious groups absolutely condemn the use of alcohol. While respecting these communities, the Catholic tradition has generally held that the use of alcohol in and of itself is neither morally right nor morally wrong. Certainly, there have been and are now outstanding Catholics who totally abstain from alcohol in a spirit of self-denial and as a work of atonement for the widespread abuses in society. Their example is praiseworthy. But Catholic morality accepts the ambiguity of the Book of Sirach, which testifies that "wine has been the ruin of many" but also that "wine is very life to man if taken in moderation" (Sirach 31:25, 27).

The moral problem here comes with the excessive use of alcohol. Drunkenness is part of the deadly sin of gluttony. By definition, drunkenness means drinking to excess, drinking to the point of losing control of one's physical and mental capacities. Saint Thomas points out that "drunkenness is a mortal sin because then a person willingly and knowingly deprives himself or herself of the use of reason."

Eddie is a sophomore at a major university. He is a fairly good student and a very good athlete. He was sitting in on the round-table discussion about the resurgence of heavy drinking on campus. Eddie's voice had a defiant edge to it: "I'm a party animal, not a do-gooder. I like to get drunk. I like to be stoned. I'm not an alcoholic. I drink only when I want to, only on weekends. I don't let alcohol interfere with my studies or my sports." Eddie is probably in for some rude awakenings as he gets older, but for now he seems not to mind how he degrades and debases his own human dignity by drunkenness. Chances are good that he, like too many other people, doesn't mind driving while drunk either, ignoring the serious risk of harming other people.

While people like Eddie willingly and knowingly abuse alcohol and commit the sin of drunkenness, other people are powerless over alcohol and drink out of compulsion. Such people are called alcoholics. Alcoholism is a vast and complex topic and cannot be covered in depth in these few pages. A body of excellent literature is available from Alcoholics Anonymous, especially the "big book" entitled: *Alcoholics Anonymous: The Story of How Many Thousands of Men and Women Recovered From Alcohol.*

Alcoholism is generally considered a sickness that affects body, mind, and soul. John C. Ford, a longtime expert in this field, describes alcoholism as "the general disordered condition of those who have been addicted to grave excess in the use of alcoholic beverages over a long period of time. Also called alcoholism at times is the excessive drinking itself, to the extent that it is marked by a lack of control. In either case alcoholism is a behavior as well as a medical or psychiatric problem. It should be distinguished from mere drunkenness, in which the element of compulsion or addiction is absent."[4] Alcoholism is a widespread sickness, embracing over twelve million people in the United States and affecting millions of others who are relatives, friends, employers of the alcoholic.

TEMPERANCE

The obvious virtue that must be exercised to combat excesses in the use of food and drink is the virtue of temperance (moderation). It demands that we take an honest look at our drinking and eating habits and that we exercise self-discipline over them. It is all too easy to drift into destructive patterns in these areas and gradually to abandon any real discipline over them. We will readily find excuses for these excesses (stress, worry, fun) but never any *good* reasons. The life-giving virtue of temperance enables us to take charge of our lives, to practice moderation and responsibility in these matters. The virtue of temperance means "knowing when to say when." With honest effort and the grace of God, the life-giving virtue of temperance can be attained.

In the case of the alcoholic, the best hope for recovery lies in the tried-and-true program of Alcoholic Anonymous. This splendid organization has a proven plan for dealing with alcoholism. The plan demands total abstinence from alcohol — a frightening prospect to the alcoholic — but also provides a support system in regular meetings and many wise strategies for attaining and maintaining sobriety. A.A. has been instrumental in rescuing millions of people from the sickness of alcoholism and returning them to a free and productive way of life. Help for the alcoholic, once he or she admits the need for help, is only a phone call away.

In the case of those who are guilty of excess in the area of food, temperance in the form of moderation and the proper use of treatment centers are likewise important, as indicated above.

One other area that demands moderation is the use of drugs other than alcohol. This is a bewildering area of modern life and morality. In what seems like a very short period of time, the United States has become what experts call a "drug culture." All of a sudden a major "war on drugs" has to be fought on many fronts and with no assurance of victory.

For the sake of simple analysis, we should note that psychotropic or psychoactive drugs are chemicals that influence the working of the mind and alter behavior, mood, and mental functioning. These drugs may be divided into two main categories: therapeutic and nontherapeutic.

Therapeutic drugs fall into three main categories: (a) antipsychotic drugs, sometimes called major tranquilizers, are used to treat major mental illnesses, such as schizophrenia and paranoia, by suppressing the symptoms and helping the person to cope; (b) antidepressant drugs are used to stimulate the central nervous system and provide relief for depression; (c) antianxiety drugs, or minor tranquilizers, are used to combat stress and anxiety.

From a moral viewpoint the use of therapeutic drugs is justified provided they are used under the direction of a competent physician and are believed to be for the total welfare of the patient. For the sick and suffering, many of these drugs are great gifts of God. Without them, some people would not be able to function in a truly human way.

Nontherapeutic drugs are used not for reasons of health but for purposes of pleasure, self-transcendence, recreation, and the like. Through these drugs people seek a feeling of elation, euphoria, relaxation. In the United States, some of these drugs, such as alcohol and nicotine, are legal. Others, such as cocaine, crack (the powerful smokable form of cocaine), heroin, and marijuana, are illegal. The "war on drugs" is aimed at the latter, not only at the users but also at the manufacturers and distributors as well.

It seems more and more clear that these illegal drugs constitute a major health danger. Used in sufficient quantity and with sufficient regularity, they can exert damaging effects on the mind and body. Moreover, they pose the danger of addiction and the whole range of immoral behavior (such as violent crime) which addiction gives rise to. Certainly, Christians who take seriously their responsibility for care of their health will want to avoid these illegal drugs. If addicted, they will take the painful steps to freedom from the addiction.

There are, to be sure, many reasons for the widespread use of drugs in our society and the addiction that so easily follows. But one dimension of the problem that is often casually dismissed is the spiritual dimension. When we speak of the forces that move people to drugs and addiction, we are speaking of the ancient scourges of the human spirit and the age-old hungers of the human heart.

As human persons, we are, after all, more than party animals. We have deep spiritual psychic needs: the need for love and belonging, for self-esteem and acceptance by others, for creativity and knowledge and beauty. And, yes, a need for God. When these needs are not met — in our families, our relationships, our jobs or careers, our culture — we experience a great void and go searching for something that will fill the emptiness and ease the pain.

This search, as experience records, goes down many byways. In one way or another, all of the deadly sins are involved in this search. One of the byways is the use of drugs. There is always a new hope that drugs will bring the fulfillment we are searching for. Of course, they never do. From a Christian viewpoint, any successful "war on drugs" will have to help people meet their fundamental spiritual needs which too often are not being met in our society. And this is true of all the "children" of the deadly sin of gluttony treated in this chapter.

Reflection/Discussion Questions

1. From your own experience and observation, how would you describe the deadly sin of gluttony in our society at this time?
2. Do you think that Christian people, especially young people, fully understand the importance of temperance or moderation in their lives?
3. Share any suggestions you may have for fighting the "war on drugs" in one's own family.
4. In your opinion, is the spiritual dimension of human nature sufficiently recognized in trying to deal with food and drug addictions?

NOTES

[1]Dennis McBride, *The Gospel of Luke,* p. 219.

[2]See *Economic Justice for All: Pastoral Letter on Catholic Social Teaching and the U.S. Economy,* (Washington, DC: National Conference of Catholic Bishops, 1986) Chapter 3, Part C.

[3]Kenneth Guentert, "Gluttony: Love at First Bite," *U.S. Catholic,* August 1987, p. 12-13.

[4]John C. Ford, "Alcoholism," *New Catholic Encyclopedia.*

CHAPTER EIGHT

Lust

"God did not call us to impurity."

(1 THESSALONIANS 4:7)

Chastity

"Therefore glorify God in your body."

(1 CORINTHIANS 6:20)

J anet was an attractive, well-dressed woman of twenty-four. She was taking stock of her life. Her main problem, she felt, was a promiscuous attitude toward sex. She confided that during her college years she was sexually active with many different men. She didn't pretend that she loved any of them. Moreover, she didn't really experience a strong feeling of intimacy or even pleasure in these encounters. Looking back, she was also quite surprised that she never even thought of the possibility of contracting a venereal disease. Though she didn't know her partners well, she assumed they didn't have herpes or AIDS.

As Janet examined her motives and actions, a number of serious questions arose for her: Why am I so promiscuous? Is it because I love myself or hate myself? What does sex mean to me? Why do I so easily separate sex from love? Does my behavior say that I may even have self-destructive feelings? How do I begin to change my attitudes?

These and other similar questions cannot be answered briefly or simply; but some of them can be profitably examined in the broader context of the deadly sin of lust and the life-giving virtue of chastity. In this chapter — after examining the true meaning of sex — we will address the problem of lust and then acclaim the virtue of chastity.

LUST

Since the sin of lust is the abuse of sex, we must first examine the two different views on the meaning of sex. The word *sex* is commonly used in two distinct senses: (1) to indicate the specific qualities, physical and psychological, which make a person either male or female; and (2) to describe sexually motivated desires or behavior.

In the first sense, sex is an extremely important ingredient of the human person. "According to contemporary scientific research, the human person is so profoundly affected by sexuality that it must be considered as one of the factors which give to each person's life the principal traits that distinguish it."[1]

In this profound sense, sex may be described as the way of being and relating to the world as a male or female person. Men and women, in every aspect of their being, experience themselves and relate to others in a distinctly male or female way.

From a Christian perspective, men and women "image" God through their sexuality.

God created man in his image;
in the divine image he created him;
male and female he created them.

(Genesis 1:27)

Sexuality "is that aspect of personhood which makes us capable of entering into loving relationships with others. Theology teaches that relationship — the gift of self to another — is at the very heart of God. The Father and the Son give themselves totally to one another and the mutuality of their total response in love is the Holy Spirit, binding them together. We honor God and become more like him when we create in our lives the loving, other-centered relationships which at the same time give us such human satisfaction and personal fulfillment...."[2]

In addition, sexuality is an aspect of human personality by which we relate affectively to others. It is a relational power which includes the qualities of sensitivity, understanding, warmth, openness to persons, compassion, and mutual support. These are the qualities we associate with a loving man or woman.

In the second sense mentioned above, sex refers to genital or venereal pleasure. It refers to the physical, organic expression of sex through the act of sexual intercourse and those acts that are naturally related to it. It refers to sexual arousal in the genital organs, whether partial or complete (that is, orgasm), as well as the intense pleasure that goes with it. It refers, even more basically, to the "sexual appetite" or "sexual drive" which impels the human person — through desires, fantasies, urges — to seek genital or venereal pleasure.

Two Views of Sex

In the course of the centuries, individuals and societies have tended to take one of two views of sex and genital pleasure. These views are rooted in larger "world-views" of philosophies and theologies about the human person, the body, the purposes of sexual pleasure, and the like.

One view goes like this:
Spirit is good, matter is evil;
the soul is pure, the body is corrupt;
love is beautiful, sex is shameful.

The other view is quite different:
The spirit doesn't matter, the body is supreme;
self-control is negative, pleasure is positive;
love is irrelevant, sex is meaningful.

While these two views are not mutually exclusive at any moment of history, it seems to be true that one view dominates at any given time. In our American culture at this particular time, the second view dominates. It is sometimes described as the "American sex revolution" or the "Playboy and Playgirl" philosophy of life. Basic to this view is the conviction that genital pleasure should be sought for its own sake; there is no reason to link such pleasure with love or commitment; there should be no restraint on venereal activities, no matter how promiscuous or dehumanizing they may be.

Faces of Lust

Lust may be defined as the disordered or unrestrained seeking of genital pleasure. Lust is not sinful because it is connected with sex or because it is pleasurable, but precisely because it is disordered or "irrational," that is, against the order of reason. Lust, according to Saint Thomas, pits the "lower powers" of passion and animal instincts against the "higher powers," the distinctively human faculties of reason and will.

Lust is fueled by concupiscence, one of the results of original sin. In this context concupiscence means that the desires of the flesh are not automatically subject to reason and will and grace. "The lust of the flesh," writes Pope John Paul II, "is a permanent element of man's fallen nature." Thomas Merton believed that sexual appetites were the most difficult of all natural appetites to control and tended to "completely blind the human spirit to all interior light." Because of concupiscence, there is a strong tendency for men and women to turn true, other-centered sexual love into a mere self-centered satisfaction.

Speaking of the Fall from grace as described in Genesis, Ralph Martin rightly points out: "When our first parents exchanged the truth of God for a serpent's lie, the male-female relationship was seriously wounded. God's good gift of sexual desire was distorted by lust, self-deception, selfishness, guilt."[3] Gilbert K. Chesterton used to say that even if we did not have a clear theology of original sin, we would know from experience, and especially from experience of the tangled web of male-female relationships, that something had gone wrong with the human race. Would not many men and women who have been hurt by the power of lust readily bear that out?

Like all the deadly sins, lust has certain "offspring." Some of the children of lust, according to Saint Thomas, are blindness of mind or perversion of heart, rashness, inconstancy, inordinate self-love. Lust invites us to close our eyes to our values, to harden our hearts against the needs of others, to pursue genital pleasure for its own sake without weighing the consequences, to focus so much on our own satisfaction that other moral instincts are pushed aside.

The deadly sin of lust is an offense against ourselves, against other persons, against society.

- *Against ourselves:* Lust is a kind of slavery in which the person is in bondage to uncontrolled passions and desires and fantasies. Lust is evil, remarks Karl Menninger, not because it is about sex or pleasure "but because it corrupts or destroys the personality of the participants."[4] The corrupting force of lust is often passed over in our society, but in private many people are willing to testify that they are powerless over their sexual urges and that they have sacrificed some of their most tender human feelings because of the power of lust.

- *Against other persons:* "In lust," states Vincent Genovese, "I am concerned with the fulfillment of my own needs and desires, with little or no thought being given to the needs, interests, and desires of the other."[5] This kind of focus on self is certainly characteristic of many expressions of lust, such as rape, incest, and pornography, as we shall mention below.
- *Against society:* There is little doubt that the fruits of lust affect the social fabric. Our society, for example, faces a veritable epidemic of children born out of wedlock, many of them to teenage girls. In addition countless other children are destroyed through abortion. Is it not lust which prompts young men and women to engage in genital acts for pleasure, while refusing to take responsibility for those acts?

Lust and Cruelty

One dimension of lust that may easily pass unnoticed is the dimension of cruelty. We may naively think that lust is all about pleasure, but more often it is all about dominance and abuse. In its blind drive to satisfy itself, lust takes advantage of the vulnerability or weakness or innocence of others. Saint Thomas says that the "parts" of lust include rape, incest, fornication, adultery.

Rape is not so much about sexual pleasure as it is about raw dominance of another. Rape is characteristically less a

90

sexual act than a form of assault — a form of hurting, debasing, and destroying another person for self-satisfaction. Likewise, sexual abuse of children, whether by members of the family (incest) or by outsiders, is an act of dominance against the powerless and the innocent. In hard-core pornography the emphasis is more often on sadism and masochism, on humiliation and conquest than it is on tenderness and mutual loving. Pornography is sometimes described as a "victimless crime." In truth, there are many victims: the traumatized child, the debased woman, the desensitized male, the destroyed marriage.

Adultery, too, is a kind of violence: not physical violence but emotional violence. It is a violation of trust and fidelity; it is a sin that breaks promises and hearts. In its own way, it especially does violence to the self-image and security of young children.

Fornication or nonmarital sex is widely accepted as an act of love, but is it really? Janet (mentioned at the opening of this chapter) was honest in not pretending to love the men with whom she slept. Lustful people are seldom so honest. They manipulate and seduce others into a genital relationship, but they do not necessarily love or even care about the other person as an individual. Lust involves no real choice of a partner, nor does it take responsibility for the consequences of its acts.

CHASTITY

"We are by nature sexual beings, endowed with specifically sexual desires or drives. Some regulation of our sexual appetite is required by the nature of human life, both personal and social. When we apprehend self-moderation and self-regulation as inherently right or good, they assume a moral character and become the natural virtue of chastity."[6] The life-giving virtue of chastity is, then, the virtue that moderates and regulates the sexual appetite or genital pleasure according to the principles of right reason and the law of God.

Though commonly considered a negative and restrictive virtue, chastity is much more than that. It is aimed at attaining higher and more positive goals. It is a virtue which concerns the whole personality with regard to both interior and exterior behavior. The heart of chastity, as James Bacik has pointed out, is respect. "If we acquire the general habit of respecting persons as individuals, then it is less likely that we will exploit them as sexual objects. This sense of justice attunes people to the destructive consequences of any sexual activity that is dominating, manipulative, and abusive...."[7] Chastity liberates the human person from the bondage of self-centered, aggressive, manipulative sexual activity.

For the Christian, moreover, chastity is concerned not only with moderation of sexual pleasure, it is intimately related to love and holiness: "This is the will of God, your holiness: that you refrain from immorality, that each of you know how to acquire a wife for himself in holiness and honor, not in lustful passion as do the Gentiles who do not know God..." (1 Thessalonians 4:3-5). "Be imitators of God, as beloved children, and live in love, as Christ loved us....Immorality or any impurity or greed must not even be mentioned among you, as is fitting among holy ones, no obscenity or silly or suggestive talk, which is out of place, but instead, thanksgiving" (Ephesians 5:1-4).

Basic Beliefs About Chastity

The life-giving virtue of chastity is governed by several basic beliefs.

The first of these is that sex is a good gift of God to men and women. "God looked at everything he had made, and he found it very good" (Genesis 1:31). The recurrent heresy that sex is evil, the body shameful, pleasure wrong, must be rejected.

Second, sex is an important gift of God. It is important for the individual person, for the family, and for society. Because it is important, it should be taken seriously and treated with respect. It should not be trivialized as it is repeatedly in movies and TV shows and ads. Nor should it be brutalized as it is in pornography and obscenity. "For ultimately sex and sexuality are only abstractions. The concrete reality is the sexed human being, male or female, made in the image and likeness of God. To trivialize sex, to make it a subject of jest or of little importance, is to cheapen the human person."[8]

The third fundamental belief is that God has built into human sexuality certain intrinsic meanings that cannot be erased or ignored. Among the most important of these meanings is that the sexual union of husband and wife is honorable, a special expression of their married love which reflects God's love for his people and Christ's love for the Church. The freedom and joy of sex celebrated in marriage is one of God's best gifts to his people.

But like many things human, sex is ambivalent. It can be either creative or destructive. Sexual intercourse is a moral and human good only within marriage; outside marriage it is wrong. Sexual intercourse, in the words of Pope John Paul II, is realized in a truly human and moral way "only if it is an integral part of the love by which a man and woman commit themselves totally to each other until death."

The marriage covenant itself calls for a sexual love that is faithful and exclusive — in good times and in bad, in sickness and in health. Adultery is a direct attack on this faithful and exclusive love. By adultery the truth of sexual love in marriage is betrayed.

The American bishops have pointed out a truth that most of us experience on a daily basis: "Our society gives considerable encouragement to premarital and extramarital sexual relations as long as, it is said, 'no one gets hurt.' But this casual and irresponsible attitude toward sexual relations is not worthy of beings created in God's image and made adopted children nor are they according to God's will....Though tenderness and concern may sometimes be present, there is an underlying tendency toward exploitation and self-deception. Such relations trivialize sexuality and erode the possibility of making deep, lifelong commitments."[9]

Demands and Rewards of Chastity

Chastity is a demanding virtue because it is concerned with powerful, sometimes chaotic, forces in the human person. The urge toward sexual-genital pleasure is very strong. Even deeply committed Christians experience the schizoid intensity of lust, which at times seems to have a life of its own. Saint Paul's struggle comes to mind: "What I do, I do not understand. For I do not do what I want, but I do what I hate....So, then, I discover the principle that when I want to do right, evil is at hand" (Romans 7:15, 21). The virtue of chastity certainly calls for courage and fortitude in daily life.

Though demanding, chastity is also a liberating virtue. It sets us free from the dehumanizing lusts which we experience. It frees us from the slavery of self-centeredness. Paul recognized there was a way out of this painful conflict. "The law of the spirit of life in Christ Jesus has freed you from the law of sin and death" (Romans 8:2). Paul invites his listeners not to be discouraged by the struggle against the "wiles of the devil," but to stand firm in watchful prayer and self-denial.

Reflection/Discussion Questions

1. Do you think that most people have a positive or a negative attitude toward sex?
2. Name and discuss some of the common ways in which sex is trivialized in modern society.
3. If you were trying to describe the deadly sin of lust to a group of freshmen in high school, what points would you especially try to make?
4. Does the virtue of chastity, as taught by the Catholic Church, make sense to you? Or do you think it is outmoded? Explain your position.

NOTES

[1]Congregation for the Doctrine of the Faith, *Declaration on Sexual Ethics,* 1976, #1.

[2]Bishop Francis Mugavero, *Sexuality: God's Gift,* p.2.

[3]Ralph Martin, *Servant Ministries Newsletter,* October 1988, p. 1.

[4]Karl Menninger, *Whatever Became of Sin?* (New York: E.P. Dutton Publishers, 1973), p. 140.

[5]Vincent Genovese, S.J., *In Pursuit of Love: Catholic Morality and Human Sexuality,* (Wilmington, DE: M. Glazier, 1987), p. 153.

[6]Sean O'Riordan, C.SS.R., "Chastity," *New Catholic Encyclopedia.*

[7]James Bacik, "Lust: It Can't Be Wrong When It Feels So Right," *U.S Catholic,* August 1987, p. 11.

[8]James Hanigan, *What Are They Saying About Sexual Morality?* (New York: Paulist Press, 1982), p. 4.

[9]National Council of Catholic Bishops, *To Love Christ Jesus,* p. 19.

Selected Bibliography

Aquinas, Saint Thomas. *The Summa,* Three Volumes, New York: Benzinger, 1947. The main treatment of sins and virtues is in Volume Two.

Capps, Donald. *Deadly Sins and Saving Virtues,* Philadelphia: Fortress Press, 1987.

Fairlie, Henry. *The Seven Deadly Sins Today,* Notre Dame: University of Notre Dame Press, 1979.

Häring, Bernard. *The Law of Christ,* Three Volumes, Westminster, Maryland: Newman Press, 1965.

Hanigan, James. *What Are They Saying About Sexual Morality?* New York: Paulist Press, 1982.

Menninger, Karl. *Whatever Became of Sin?* New York: E.P. Dutton Publishers, 1973.

Merton, Thomas. *New Seeds of Contemplation,* New York: New Direction Books, 1961.

Norquist Gustin, Marilyn. *Jesus' Pattern for a Happy Life: The Beatitudes,* Liguori, MO: Liguori Publications, 1981.

Tavris, Carol. *Anger: The Misunderstood Emotion,* New York: Simon and Shuster, 1982.